3/21 ~9

Make That
Baby
Happy!

How a "Woman in Blue" Built Hope
for Women and Children in Haiti

Barbara A. Walker

WESTBOW
PRESS®
A DIVISION OF THOMAS NELSON
& ZONDERVAN

Dedication

To the people in my life that were the building blocks to my missionary career: Norman and Dorice Brickman, who set an example of love and compassion for me to follow, Hank and Polly Glynn, who introduced me to missions, Robert Wojnarowski, who provided spiritual guidance and encouragement. Joseph R Hurston, Dr. Steve Henley, and Sister Mary Cabrini who invited me to participate in mission work with them in over 25 countries, and my daughters Colleen and Arlene who encouraged me and supported my work in Haiti.

CONTENTS

Foundations

It Takes a Village

Location, Location, Location

Make That Baby Happy!

Fellow missionaries, Sandra and Jane, have described BARBARA as:

It Can't Get Worse

The Other Side of Adoption

Perspectives

INTRODUCTION

Twins born in our mud hut village were not doing well and my wife, Cindy, and I could do nothing to help them. I was on a hurricane relief flight and Cindy was leaving Haiti for the U.S. At the airport, Cindy ran into Barbara Walker and told her about the babies. Cindy pleaded with Barb to go get the little ones and find a good home for them. Barb accepted the mission, but one of the twins died before she arrived. Barbara nursed the surviving twin to health, called her Baby Ruth, and found a home for her. That's how I first met Barb. Barbara rescues babies. There's no one better! She's fierce when it comes to her mission. As a matter of fact, I call her "Rambo in the Blue Dress." She is absolutely fearless and determined when it comes to rescuing babies.

Our mission organization, Air Mobile Ministries, responds to major disasters. When Cindy can't join me, she urges me to take Barb. "She'll bring you home alive," she says with a smile. Barb has been an invaluable team member, helping us place nearly 350 life-saving water purifiers throughout Haiti, and assisting us on disaster relief missions around the world.

When we took water purifiers to Myanmar following a devastating cyclone, a customs officer seemed intent on seizing the life-saving instruments. Barb went in her "crazy babbling fool" routine and so overwhelmed the officer that he quickly urged us to just take the purifiers and go. Barb is an absolute genius when facing certain defeat.

Another time, in Haiti, 12-14 heavily armed men ambushed us. While I was calling on the name of Jesus, Barb was beating one of the gangsters to a pulp. Jesus came through and rescued us and saved the gangster from a terrible beating. That's why I call her "Rambo in the Blue Dress!"

Cindy and I have adopted two girls whom Barb rescued. Neither would likely be alive today had Barb not reached in and pulled these little ones out of a dire situation. Our Lord must have had a very good time when he formed Barb in her mother's womb. I suspect that he had a big smile on his face when he made Barb. Cindy and I are eternally grateful to our Lord for bringing Barb into our lives and so are thousands of others who have been touched by this fierce and courageous woman of God.

Joe Hurston

PROLOGUE

During my first visit to Haiti, I often stood in my room and looked out a window at a small chicken coop. The coop was about two feet wide, three feet long and had a roof peak of about three feet. It resembled a small dog house. The rooster that lived there awakened me each morning with loud crowing.

I wondered how this rooster survived. Chickens, goats, dogs, cats, and rats wandered Port-au-Prince streets scavenging food and water from the garbage piles, but this lone rooster, locked in a coop, had limited food and water resources.

As I worried over the welfare of the rooster, the Lord showed me that here, in Haiti, this rooster didn't have it so bad. He had a home with a roof for protection from sun and rain and he was safe from harm. Unlike this rooster, thousands of children in Port-au-Prince lived on the streets, picked through garbage for food and had no shelter from the elements or preying street people. Hungry, sick, diseased and lonely the little ones died on the streets and their bodies were carted away and buried in unmarked graves. Even those who had a shelter, were often crammed with 8-10 others into an 8' x 8' house. When you compared the accommodations of tens of thousands of Port-au-Prince children to the rooster's coop **the rooster had it pretty good!**

The image of a rooster living a better life than a child would not go away. That image changed the direction and purpose of my life.

FOUNDATIONS

He will be the sure foundation for your times, a rich store of salvation and wisdom and knowledge (Isaiah 33:6)

CHAPTER 1

No Special Plans

Is there a plan for each of our lives? Can we be observant enough to see the signs and patterns to predict what a child will be in adult life?

As a child, I was a loner. I spent much of my time playing in the woods and fields, climbing trees, picking flowers and bringing home stray animals. From the start I was a caretaker. My charges included baby birds that had fallen from their nests, wild bunnies, orphaned baby raccoons, turtles that had wandered far from a pond—and a skunk. Of course, there were always dogs and cats, and puppies and kittens. The older I got, the bigger the pets got. Lambs, treated like babies, wore diapers and drank from bottles. Piglets stumbled around with splints on their legs and half-dead calves rose on unsteady feet and began to walk after I cared for them. Observers might have predicted I would choose a caretaking profession such as doctor, nurse or veterinarian, but I had no special plans for my life.

I just lived life as it came. I don't ever remember thinking or saying what I wanted to be when I grew up. My ever broadening role as caretaker and guardian of the helpless was not shaped by textbooks and college courses but by real life. I married and had three daughters. During their early years we ran a small farm; raised cows, pigs, goats, sheep, horses, rabbits, turkeys, ducks, pheasants, and many other animals. My girls were always so busy milking the cow, cleaning the barn, or stacking hay that they didn't have time to get into trouble. The girls, though, never lacked anything and they participated in all kinds of extracurricular programs. I drove a school bus for twelve years so I was often the chauffer to their school activities. If they wanted or needed something, we just found more work to do so we could buy what they needed.

No job was too small or too big for us. We detasseled corn to produce hybrid seed corn, did commercial cleaning, landscaping, mowing, and catering. We hosted home parties and sold all kinds of merchandise and made crafts to sell at flea markets and county fairs. We worked together to build a good life. Working for what they needed or wanted instilled a strong work ethic in my daughters' lives and prepared us all for greater works ahead.

Darlene, who is married with one boy, is a registered nurse. Colleen is married with three children and has assisted me in Reach Out to Haiti. Arlene is single, and works for American Airlines in Richmond, Virginia, which has provided me the wonderful blessing of reduced airfares.

Although my main priority was caring for my children, I extended caretaking beyond my family. That care ranged from picketing and lobbying to save the unborn to visiting the elderly who had been forgotten or abandoned by family.

A thread of dependence

With all the many hats I wore, no one among my family, friends and neighbors would have suggested that I would put on a missionary hat. Unknown to me, God was fitting my head for that hat. Through those extremely busy years God was preparing me to live in a country that would require doing a wide range of tasks and handling chaotic situations — all without the basic necessities found in a developed country.

Along with the desire to help others and the love of working at many tasks, God had woven a *thread of dependence* on him into my life. My Irish Catholic mother and my Protestant father never attended church, but they sent me to a Catholic school and church. My father was possibly more spiritual than I had believed him to be because after he died, I found a very old and used Bible in his workshop. He spent most evenings in his shop and I believe he was reading the Bible part of that time.

During the difficult years of my youth, I found peace through praying, but my spiritual life didn't really develop until I was almost 40 years old.

Guided toward an unseen purpose

In 1983, God led me to attend a church in Troy, New York. The pastor, Bob Wojnarowski, is the most God-inspired preacher I have ever met. After a short time of soul searching, God led me to be re-baptized into the family of God. That was the beginning of the Holy Spirit's influence on my life. I praise the Lord for the teaching I received during the next ten years which prepared me for the work he had predestined for me. I not only learned about God, I took an active part in the ministry of the church. I worked with the audio, video, and book libraries and recorded church services. On the church property I was in charge of landscaping and assisted in snow removal. I even started a cemetery on the church grounds.

It may sound morbid, but my favorite job was doing cemetery work and burials. We dug graves, mainly by hand, and buried almost 1000 people in several cemeteries. We sold grave stones, cared for the cemetery and made Christmas blankets for graves. I even helped Oakwood Bible Church in New York build a

312-plot cemetery behind the church for church members and poor people who could not afford burial. What better time to reach out with care than when a family faces death. Little did I know that my future would involve working with people who faced death on a regular basis.

God's preparation and movement of my life toward a yet-unseen purpose was gradual. Had he said, "Go to Haiti, nurse dying children back to health and find homes for them," I would have said, "Who? Me? I don't think so!"

"...Use whatever gift you have received..."

In the early 1980's a serious illness and long recovery forced me to retire from full-time employment. This, however, gave me more time to serve our Lord. The first major move toward a new purpose in life came through *One Mission Society* (OMS formerly known as Oriental Missionary Society). I had recovered my health and decided to go on a mission trip with Men for Missions. Men for Missions (both men and women) is a layperson organization of OMS that does short-term mission projects such as construction, evangelism, medical clinics, etc.

As I considered which type of mission trip would be best for me, my past training settled the issue. I would go on a construction team. My grandfather and my father were builders. I was the fourth of six girls born to a general contractor in Albany, New York. I jokingly refer to myself as the only "boy" my parents had. I, like most children, loved the special attention that fathers gave. At a very young age I discovered the way to **my father's** heart was by working with him and developing my skills as a painter, plumber, carpenter, landscaper, and by learning other building crafts. As a result of working with my father I had developed a love and talent for construction.

I first went with OMS to Brazil in February of 1986, and then again in February of 1987 to build a church in Paranavaí. In February of 1988 we built a church in Astorga, Brazil. I also helped restore a dilapidated missionary compound in Columbia. At this time in my life, I was driven by the scripture in I Peter 4:10. "Each of you should use whatever gift you have received to serve others." I believed God was telling me to use my God-given talents and skills to help others in need. I had a working knowledge of all facets of construction and found great personal satisfaction in helping build churches in Brazil. After four trips to Brazil, a *developing* nation, I decided to step out of my comfort zone and go to an *under-developed nation* – Haiti. I was never able to get back into the comfort box after that trip.

CHAPTER 2

Surveys

An ordinary woman, the daughter of a carpenter, travelled to Haiti on a simple mission to help build a church building. Never would she have thought that a glimpse of God's blueprint would be part of this trip.

On my first trip to Haiti, I traveled with a mainline Christian organization in a group of about ten people from different states and religious denominations. The two-week trip was spent with missionaries who showed us their ministries and gave us a tour of Haiti. As on many faith-based tours to Haiti, the missionaries controlled the experience and our exposure to the realities of Haiti. Those tours are seldom controlled to hide anything, but rather to protect naïve and gullible do-gooders who can quickly find themselves in trouble or danger.

Everyone I came in contact with wanted to know more about Jesus. Wow! What a wonderful opportunity to witness to others. People clamored for the Christian tracts and Bibles in their languages of French and Creole and asked for more. I couldn't help but think what a great place for the new Christian to come. It would be like a kindergarten class of witnessing for baby Christians. Unlike, in the US where free tracts and scriptures were ignored or trampled on the ground, the people in Haiti couldn't get enough scriptures. This would be just what new Christians needed to build up their confidence and encourage the development of their witnessing skills.

Soon my two weeks were over and I announced to the group leader that I would not be returning to the States with the rest of the group. I wanted to stay in Haiti and get a better look at the real Haiti. Since I was self-supporting, I could be what I called a "missionary to the missionaries."

I stayed and filled in as hostess at guest houses, did driving, shopping, picked up mail at the airport, gathered supplies, and kept my eyes open for new ways that I could lighten the work burden for mission staffs. Living in Haiti's stifling climate and surrounded by poverty, sickness, violence, filth and political unrest can be overwhelming, so during the first months of working there, I tried to encourage and uplift the missionaries with friendly words and understanding. The words of I Peter 4:10 that had given me purpose in Brazil seemed even more meaningful as I worked in Haiti. *"Each of you should use whatever gift you have received to serve others."*

Although I sponsored and helped families with rent and medical care, I wanted to do more. On my own, I tried all sorts of ideas to help the Haitian people.

After returning to the States for a while, I came back to Haiti with typewriters and sewing machines so people could make money by typing letters and making school uniforms. I even supplied looms and yarn and taught girls, boys, women, and men how to weave placemats to sell. Often we all worked together to produce marketable items.

I never had a big plan or goal to be a full-time missionary. I was very content to work day-by-day, doing whatever needed doing, but I spent hours praying to God to show me the true needs of the Haitian people and how I could help them. I wasn't sure how I could help, but I knew I wanted to do my best to make a change in people's lives.

In 1989, I established *Reach Out To Haiti, Inc.*, a nonprofit, multi-functioning USA 501 C3 organization. *Reach Out to Haiti* partnered with several mission organizations to provide help and guidance to a variety of groups of people. The goal was to **reach out** to people in need of help, education, compassion, and, guidance. I had no plans or ambition to start a big mission organization. All I had was the burden God placed on one person to make a difference. I couldn't change a country but I could make a difference in one life at a time.

Did I really want to see ...?

My eyes began to open. I began to see the truth. Poverty and sadness, defeat and suffering surrounded and overwhelmed me. The first thing that I noticed was the children. The children I had seen in churches were clean and dressed beautifully. But here, on the streets, they wore rags or ran naked through the garbage strewn streets. I looked for smiles and laughter but found very few. I saw no toys, just children poking with sticks at discarded plastic bottles, or other assorted refuse. I also noticed that almost every child jumped at the opportunity to beg, especially from white people. I quickly realized that they were hungry and thirsty. I saw children drinking their own urine or muddy water from the puddles at the side of the road. Almost every child had a runny nose and visible open sores. Where were their parents? Why would they let them beg in the streets? I couldn't help but wonder how many of them were run over by cars or just got sick and lay dead in the street. It was almost too much for me to see. I had prayed that God would open my eyes but I didn't really want to see this.

I kept praying to God to give me understanding of the problems and how I could help the Haitian people. As soon as I thought I understood the problems, I realized that I didn't have a clue to the underlying problems or a solution. I often asked myself, "What can one person do to bring change to Haiti? Where does one start?"

In my search for ways to serve, I often painted shabby orphanages. As I painted I saw the children eating the same food each day, scraping their bowls clean and always looking for more to fill their empty stomachs. They didn't like or dislike the food. It was simply sustenance. They seldom smiled and laughter was an uncommon sound. Were they happy? I don't know. They didn't have much to be happy about. Yes, they were no longer foraging on the streets and had shelter from the elements, but I thought, "An orphanage is no place for children. Children need parents, a family, laughter and happiness. Children need love, encouragement, hugs and kisses. They are God's children and they need to know God's love, as well as that of a godly family. What could one person do?" I kept wondering.

In search of criminals

In my search for answers I found myself acting like a detective looking for crimes and the criminals. Surely, someone was to blame for the atrocities I was seeing. I prayed for God's wisdom so that I would see the truth and not judge unjustly, and that I would be open to see the failures and successes of the people that were serving God.

How could the government let this happen? Why weren't the churches and missionary groups helping the children? These questions only led to more searching for the truth. To me, the plight of these children was CRIMINAL! I could see the crime, but who were the criminals? Perhaps you think that the words crime and criminal are too harsh to be used, but I will assure you they are not. It is an obvious crime when farm animals and pets in the US are living a better life than most of the children in Haiti. The children of Haiti faced a horrible life of neglect, suffering, hunger, and desperation, only to get sick and die from something that could be cured easily with a bit of care and medicine. I felt helpless— and angry.

I began my search for the "criminals." One search led to another and I soon realized that the government in Haiti is barely functional. The only word to describe what we are led to believe is a working democratic system of government is anarchy. The government is a forceful, self-serving, morally crippled group of people trying to get rich at the expense of the people of Haiti. Without a doubt, the government is not going to help the children of Haiti.

Next, I started visiting some of the orphanages. The first one was good—too small, too poor, and overfilled, but it had a caring staff that really loved the children. The children had beds, food, clothes, and medicine, and a Christian way of life. I was able to help them a bit and still, years later I consider them to be doing a good work. My second experience, however, was horrible. Children lived in filth and showed orange-haired signs of malnutrition. To my dismay, I found that many orphanage directors used photos of the suffering children to raise money for personal use, but neglected and even abused the children.

While some orphanages in Haiti do provide adequate care I went away from my research convinced that adoption was a better solution for the children. While I saw adoption as an alternative to living on the street or living in some of the horrendous orphanages that I visited, I had no knowledge or experience of the adoption process.

I could not shake the image of the "rooster who lived better than many of the children." I felt I must do something to help the children.

Children! What an ironic surprise to see where God's path was leading me. I never was the type of woman who was obsessed with babies. I didn't beg to hold people's infants or play with toddlers. I used to tell people "I drove a school bus for over twelve years. I really don't like children anymore."

I kept praying for wisdom about how I could help the Haitian people and lived each day using my talents to serve the people. Gradually, parts of God's plan and purpose for me in Haiti became clear. It was as if God gave me glimpses of his blueprints and unfolded a section at a time for me to work on.

CHAPTER 3

Early Blueprints

While visiting an orphanage one day, I saw a half-starved baby who was fighting for his life. Luckner Joseph's mother had died, and his father had left Luckner at the orphanage. Luckner was 18 months old and weighed nine pounds. With permission, I took him from the orphanage and cared for him until he was a healthy toddler. A couple in New York, who had prayed for a child for years wanted to give him a loving home. Putting this family together was my first experience with international adoptions.

Another of the early adoptions will always remain vivid in my mind. Missionaries Leo and Colleen, and I had stopped on a spur of the moment side trip to hand out religious tracts at the Port-au-Prince airport. There we met Cindy, a nurse, who was preparing to fly out of Haiti. Cindy had a problem. She had taken on the care of badly malnourished twins, who were being treated in what passed for a "hospital."

"Barbara," Cindy asked, "could you please check on the twins and make sure they are being cared for while I'm gone?" She went on to explain, "There are no parents, and their elderly grandmother can't care for them. There is no one else."

When I hesitated, Cindy looked me in the eyes and pleaded, "Could you **please** find a family that would adopt these tiny angels?"

When I arrived at the hospital to see the twins, I found that one had not made it. I took the other one, whom I called Baby Ruth, home with me. During the next four months, keeping Baby Ruth alive and caring for her was my main work. From the start, I felt that God had a special plan in mind for her. She began to grow and with big, beautiful eyes made people on the streets stop and stare. Some even reached out to touch her. Baby Ruth, was adopted by parents from New York who named her Elizabeth. Elizabeth matured into a beautiful intelligent young woman with enchanting eyes.

By 1990, the focus of *Reach Out to Haiti* had shifted to adoption and I became an adoption facilitator. Luke and Baby Ruth were among nearly 2000 children adopted through *Reach Out to Haiti*.

My vision was to build families by matching Haitian babies who needed homes with loving Christian families. Finding people who wanted to adopt children was easy, but adoption is a long legal battle with many requirements. I had to learn the regulations and process many papers in French. I didn't speak or read French, but kept saying, "No job is impossible when God is with you." I believed. I had faith in God.

Code compliance

As a worker in the construction industry, I understood the necessity of permits and inspections in order to build a code compliant home. In a similar way, the adoption process involved legal forms and evaluations of the children and adoptive parents.

First, was testing for disease, STDs, and especially HIV. Along with the various lab tests, came a physical check-up and a psychological evaluation. Testing and documentation took months to complete, but during that time I cared for the child, providing food, clothing, vitamins, treatment for parasites and medical care.

Few orphanages will take in HIV positive babies, but I accepted and cared for two every year. I had a special regimen of nutrition and medicine that resulted in converting many positive HIV children to negative HIV. The doctors, labs, and special nutrition is costly, but the joy and victory I received when I got the HIV negative results back made it all worth the extra I put into these unwanted babies.

The next steps in readying a child for adoption were the most frustrating – dealing with bureaucracy and the parents lack of education in order to complete the legal aspect of adoption.

In the USA, the average woman will give birth to her child in a hospital. The hospital will then present the mother with an application to fill out, stating the name chosen for the child, parents' names, date of birth, sex of the child, nationality, and address. Then the hospital will issue a hospital certificate, and the government certificate will be sent to the home after being registered with the county court house vital statistic department. This is a simple process that is performed by state employees trained to be accurate when recording the documents. Getting a birth certificate is not so simple in Haiti.

The birth certificate

Obtaining a birth certificate is the first step in the mandatory paperwork needed to process the adoption. When children are brought to *Reach Out to Haiti*, we request ID cards, electoral cards, and birth certificates for the child and parents. If the child already has a birth certificate, we need to examine it carefully to see if the dates, sex, and parents' names are correct. We also check to see if the witnesses are real people who actually witnessed the birth of the child. There is a 99% chance the information is incorrect. We examine the documents for both parents' names and the correct spelling. Often the documents have spelling errors. The best scenario would be that the ID card, the electoral card, the NIF (Numero d'Identification Fiscal), and the birth certificate all match each other. This seldom happens.

If the child does not have a birth certificate, we start the process at the local tribunal court house. We write down the child's name, date of birth, sex, location of birth, parents' names, and the names of the birth witnesses. We also note the parents' ID card numbers if available.

Next we take the child and the parents to Port-au-Prince. First stop is at the tribunal to make a correct birth certificate (*Act De Naissance*). we present the parent(s), and the paper we prepared with the correct information to the clerk at the tribunal. There are three forms to choose from: mother declaration, father declaration or a *TRI* declaration (third person authorized by law); all of which are printed on paper that is uniquely selected for the court. The length, width, weight, and watermark must be correct for the document to be legal. The clerk records the information in the court ledger book and later copies the information on the correct form. All this is done **by hand** with the clerk's own hand writing. As you know, we each have our own style of hand writing with many differences in the way we form our letters. An S, I, F, and an E with an accent are often misread and create many problems.

Several days later we receive the actual certificate, and 50% of the time we find errors. Then the certificate must be returned for a correct one to be made. Where was the mistake made? Did the clerk enter the information into the ledger correctly, and then make an error on the certificate? We must make sure corrections are made both on the certificate and in the ledger. After that, we wait for the judge to sign and stamp the certificate.

This presents another challenge. Every judge, director, and other official has a registered signature in the courts. The signature is unique and a bit of an artistic creation that must be exactly duplicated on every signed document. If not correctly signed, the document may later be challenged and considered to be a fraud.

Many times, clerks use the names of people who hang around the court house as witnesses. Before going further, we must make sure the names of real witnesses to the birth were used and not names of random strangers. The names of genuine witnesses is especially important for USA adoptions, as many times during the adoption visa process the consulate officer will request the presence of the witnesses to the birth.

Finally, we have a birth certificate that we believe is correct. This certificate now goes to the Department of Archives where we obtain the *Attestation De Signature Des Officers D'etat Civil* paper that verifies that the judge's signature is correct, and states that his signature is registered in the court. By the time we receive this paper a month or more of time has passed. This certificate is only good for one year, so we must then submit it for legalization at the Parquet Court. One to three weeks later the certificate is returned, signed and stamped and ready to be sent to the *Ministere De La Justice Department*. Again the certificate is examined to determine if the paper's signatures and stamps are legal and if so it receives another stamp and signature from that officer. This process takes one to three weeks.

Remember, at all departments only one person with a recorded certified signature may sign the paper. If this person is on vacation, or just not working for any reason, the process is stopped until the proper signature can be obtained. Note, there are 365 days in a year. If you count holidays, Saturdays and Sundays, manifestations, and government shut downs we are probably down to 150 actual work days a year, at best.

Now the certificate is taken to the department of Foreign Affairs for the last stamp and signature to make this document legal. At this point we have paid over $900 Haitian dollars to legalize this one document. Now believing the document, stamps, and signatures are all legal, the certificate is ready to join the other documents in the dossier and be submitted to IBESR the social services of Haiti.

At IBESR the dossier is examined and processed, which usually takes from one month to a year for approval. By the time the dossier is approved by the IBESR the birth certificate may have expired and a new full-page archives certificate, requiring all new legalizations will be required by the department of immigration. Back to square one. Now we hope and pray that the first clerk that recorded the birth certificate in the court ledger did it correctly the first time with no misspellings, or mistakes of both the child's and the parents' names.

This process is very difficult because not all tribunals fill up the ledger book in one year. When the ledger book is filled it must then be copied by hand for the judge so he can refer to this book in the future. The book is then sent to the Department of Parquet where it is logged in and copied for records. Then it is sent to the Department of Justice where it is again copied for records. When this is complete, then the ledger book goes to the Department of archives where it is logged in, and is placed in the library to be available to prepare the full-page archive that is needed for children over one year old requesting a passport.

Again I remind you that each entry was entered with someone's unique hand writing leaving it open to personal interpretation of each entry. Again I repeat: many, many times the hand writing, or carelessness of the person reading or recording the information presents problems. The ledger, birth certificates, and archives must all match. Too often an error shows up during this process causing more time, delay and expenses to obtain an acceptable document. Oh yes, this means you then must send this new document to the Parquet Court, Department of Justice, and Foreign Affairs for stamps and signatures again before it is legal to make the passport.

I would say that in the USA the odds of obtaining the correct birth certificate is 99% or higher. I only wish that in Haiti it was better than a 50% chance. I have been doing adoptions in Haiti since 1990 and found that until recently the USA Consulate officers were people of compassion, holding the welfare of a child as first priority. They were realistic, and aware that they were working in a third world country that does not hold their officers up to any standards of accuracy or performance. They were able to work with documents that were presented by people attempting to meet all the legal requirements, knowing that sometimes small errors were not preventable.

Little Orphan Annie

Now that I have described the agonizing quest for a correct birth certificate in Haiti, I must tell the story of my birth certificate. When I reached the age of 63, I decided to apply for a *Permis de Sejour* which allows foreigners to stay in Haiti for more than 30 days at a time.

Now remember, I had a full life before Haiti. I was born in Albany, NY, USA and lived in and around Albany for most of my life. I had a NY birth certificate that provided proof of my legal identity and a Social Security Card. I had licenses to drive passenger vehicles, school buses and vehicles that carried hazardous materials. I had a permit to carry a gun, to teach CPR and first aid, and I taught defensive driving. I had gone to school, opened bank accounts, got married, given birth to three girls, paid taxes and worked at many jobs. Later, in life, I qualified to receive social security payments from both New York State and federal governments. I held a valid USA passport, and for all of these things I had to present a legal birth certificate. When I married and applied to change my name to Barbara Ann Walker I had to produce a marriage certificate and my birth certificate.

When I applied for the *Permis de Sejour* I asked a lawyer friend to do the paperwork. I supplied photo copies of my Haitian ID (NIF card), Haiti driver's license, USA passport, birth certificate, bank statements, marriage certificate and other documents to prove my identity. Soon the lawyer called me.

"Barbara," he said, "we need the names of your mother and father."

"It's on my birth certificate," I said. "I included a translation of my birth certificate and all the information is on it."

"No, the names aren't there," he said.

I figured the translation was not accurate, so I told him the names of my parents.

Weeks went by and I received my *Permis de Sejour.* When the supporting documents were returned to me, I looked at the translation of my birth certificate and found my parents' names were not listed. Still wondering why the translator had not filled in the names, I checked it against my USA birth certificate.

To my surprise, my US birth certificate, simply stated: Barbara Ann Maki, birth; April 21 1944, female, born in Albany NY USA. No father or mother were listed. In fact the birth certificate didn't even have a place for that information.

I called my sister. "Get out your birth certificate and tell me who your father and mother were," I said. She of course thought I was crazy but read off the names of our parents as they were printed on her birth certificate.

"They always liked you best!" I told her, and explained how I had no parents listed on my birth certificate.

Determined to get to the bottom of this mystery, I checked to see if my parents were recorded in the New York State record books. They were not recorded. My daughter Colleen then went through months of phone calls and paperwork with the Vital Statistics Office, to have my parents properly registered and a new birth certificate issued to me. The Vital Statistics Office agreed to register my birth certificate with the names of my parents on it, but there was one catch. My father's name was Lauri J. Maki, but they refused to use that name on my new birth certificate. They said Lauri is now considered a common female name, so they entered my father's name as Laurence J. Maki. Yes, even in the USA mistakes are made on birth certificates.

IT TAKES A VILLAGE

You have been a refuge for the poor, a refuge for the needy in their distress, a shelter from the storm and a shade from the heat. (Isaiah 25:4)

CHAPTER 4

I Just Want Life For My Baby

After having completed hundreds of adoptions in about a ten year span, I felt compelled to do something for the unfortunate women that had to make the heart breaking decisions to place their children in my hands for adoption. Women were coming to me daily, asking me to adopt their children. I listened to their sad stories about poor living conditions, lack of medical help for their children, the desperate need for food and stories of the babies they had buried. The phrase that I heard over and over again was, "I just want life for my baby."

"Why do they keep having babies?"

The big question that everyone asked me was, "Why do the women keep having babies when they cannot provide for them?" I had been hearing the same answer, with a few variations from each lady. They came to the city in hopes of finding a better life. Most had no parents, no education, no job and no money. They soon discovered there were no available jobs in the city. Even if they had family to go home to, they had no money for the return trip. They had to make friends in the city in order to find food and a place to live. Subsequently they would move from place to place each day to find food and either sleep on the streets or in a new found friend's house. They soon became victims of people around them.

The solution to their homeless plight often came from a man who would offer to share a house and the two would begin a relationship. In Haiti, rent is paid in six-month increments and by the time the rent was due again, the woman would usually be pregnant. The man, not wanting the burden of providing for a child would move out, leaving the woman with no means to pay the next rent bill.

Now, pregnant, homeless, and with no means of support, the woman was back on the street. Even if the child was born alive it often died because the woman was too malnourished to provide milk for a nursing baby. If the child survived, the mother must find a way to sustain both her life and her child's. Seeking a way to survive, the woman would move in with another man, and become pregnant again. The cycle would repeat itself year after year with more children adding to her hopeless predicament. The surviving children were often abandoned on the streets, or left at a relative's house, or an orphanage.

Children should be a blessing and bring a feeling of love and fulfillment to a woman's life, but under these conditions, the children became a burden and brought sadness to the women. The mothers became desperate to provide for their children and love got lost in the hopeless goal of keeping the children alive. Most of these women suffer the loss of one or more children to death at birth or in infancy, bringing a sadness and depression that never goes way.

What could be done to help them? That is what I asked myself over and over again. What if someone gave some of these women a place to live without their having to provide sexual services to a man? What if these women had a home, a job and maybe some education, so they could improve their lives? What if someone just showed them some love, kindness and how to start a new way of life? Out of those questions I began to design and develop a place of refuge for single mothers.

A $10,000 faith pledge—by me!

Part of my ministry in Haiti had included building houses for several people, so I was acquainted with suppliers and acquainted with the obstacles to construction there. I stepped out in faith and made an agreement to purchase a piece of land outside of Port-au-Prince near the town of Bon Repos. The land was a swamp bordered by more swamp on two sides, but the price was $10,000 USD. The owner agreed to payments over one year. I trusted God to provide the money, but decided to do what I could to raise the money. I returned to New York where I could always find good-paying painting jobs.

While in New York, I received a phone call. "You probably don't remember me," a man said. "My name is Mr. Ruuska."

"Of course, I remember you," I answered. "You adopted two wonderful boys from me several years ago."

He then went on to tell me, "My mother-in-law recently died."

"I am sorry for your loss," I said.

"Well, the reason I'm calling is that she left us some money and we want to send a check to you. We are sending it out of love for the boys and we want to give this as a thank-you for the opportunity to adopt them."

I thought *wonderful, every little bit will help.*

"I'm sending you a check for $10,000 and you use it for whatever you wish."

I blurted out, "I can tell you right now, how it will be used!"

"You don't have to tell me how, just use it as you wish."

I went on to tell him, "God knew that I needed this money. This is the exact price I asked God to supply to purchase a tract of land to start building homes for street women."

And so, the new place for homeless mothers was named Ruuska Village in honor of its benefactors, the Ruuskas.

The village started slowly. The swampy lot was a breeding place for mosquitoes, carriers of malaria and dengue fever. We hauled many tons of fill to elevate the lot three feet above the adjacent swamp area. The houses, made of concrete block with metal roofs cost $3500USD.

Several people donated money toward the building of the houses. While building the houses, I discovered I needed a depot building to secure tools and building supplies, so some money had to be directed to that project. With two 10' x 15' houses built and the depot finished I prepared to welcome my first homeless women.

The houses sat empty for six months.

When I approached women that I had been helping and offered a free home, they responded with, "I don't know Bon Repos. I don't have any friends there."

I couldn't understand their reasoning. Many of the women were living in Cité Soleil, considered one of the biggest slums in the Northern Hemisphere. Cité Solei had been built on a garbage dump—not a smoothed over and grass planted landfill such as in the USA, but on a mud, cans, garbage, dead animal, stinking refuse area. The area had a poorly maintained open canal system that served as its sewage system. Green water and methane gas covered the ground. Children sat or played in muddy filth. With no clean water for drinking or bathing, sickness and disease were rampant. Rats, roaches, bedbugs, and swarms of fever-carrying mosquitoes never bothered to hide in the daytime. Even worse, gangs ruled the streets. Rape, kidnapping, beatings, and shootings occurred daily. Law enforcement officers would only enter the area to beat and rob the poor.

Exasperated, I said, "You didn't know Cité Solei when you came to the city! Surely living here would be better than living in that rat hole!"

Finally Mirlande Joseph and Chrislda Corrant were brave enough to move in. I then built houses Number Three and Number

Four. I thought, "Once a few people move in, others will line up at the gate to get a house. They will be so thankful to have their own home." I though, still did not understand the women's way of thinking. When I offered a home to one woman, she wrote back ... *"For the house you are giving me, I will need a bed, mug, table, chairs, stove, fan, radio and TV. If you don't have possibilities to send me everything, I will stay home. I would like to have many things before I go to the house you give me."* Eventually, she moved in, but without all of her requests.

To the women, who had only found shelter in crowded houses, the 10' x 15' houses were too big, so they invited friends and family members to move in with them. I set down one rule – NO MEN IN THE HOUSES. That meant no brothers, uncles, fathers, cousins... **no men**. This was the only means of birth control I could enforce in the little village of single women.

I tried to choose women with one or two children, but then children they had previously placed in homes of relatives started to show up. Many times the children were accompanied by sisters or cousins who joined the family. As the community of women grew, I insisted that they keep the village clean and be friendly to each other.

Years later, one Florida visitor described her first night in Ruuska village.

> *The laughter and chattering of the kids had died down and I lay in the sweltering room trying to go to sleep. I listened to the sound of the blowing fan as it labored away, poised inches from my body. Chirps from crickets in hidden corners, the occasional cry of a baby from inside a caretaker's house, the staccato voices of other women as they hung out on one or another's stoop – braiding hair, doing laundry, or just visiting in their rapid-fire Creole, were new sounds to me and kept pulling my attention away from sleep.*

The road to the peaceful setting of that night had not been easy, nor had it happened quickly.

Rules of residence

Although, the women had food, and solid concrete homes in a walled village that gave them a sense of security, it was "tough going" at the beginning. The women were used to fighting for everything they needed and they had very poor self-esteem. The women would fight each other like cats and dogs. During those early years I spent a lot of time running men out of the houses and separating cat fights where women were biting, kicking, scratching, and rolling about the yard.

I almost gave up more than once, but instead, I began training the women as you would children. Rewards were given for good behavior and punishment was given for undesirable behaviors. Rules were new to the women, but in time, most women decided that rules weren't so bad.

One of the first battles was over personal hygiene. At first, the village had a bathing room and two out-house toilets, but they didn't get used much. The women felt that they did not need toilets or a bathing room because they were used to bathing in public and would just squat anywhere in public to relieve themselves. Clothing was to wear when going to the city or church, but not necessarily at home.

Health 101—Clean water

Forty percent of the people in Haiti lack access to clean water and only one in five have access to a sanitary toilet. Additionally, the leading cause of infant mortality and illness in the children of Haiti is contaminated water. The country currently has the highest infant mortality rate in the Western Hemisphere. (water. org; haitiwater.org) *

We had water in the neighborhood, but had to carry it to the village. Although drilling a well would be costly, I knew that access to clean water on our property was essential for the health of the women and children. With a well providing adequate water we were able to add ceramic toilets and a shower room.

Boys carry water from the well to their homes.
Photography by <u>audreydewys.com</u>

Some of the women needed instruction in proper use of the facilities. I demanded that the women keep the village clean. I provided garbage cans and ensured that all garbage was removed once per week. The children were taught to keep the yard clean too. Additionally, all children, even the smallest, were to use the toilets. It took almost three years for me to win the personal hygiene and no-more-fights war. When the cat fights ended, though, a family atmosphere began growing.

The village started to become a family group. The women started to help each other and for the most part observed the rules of the village. When the women chafed at the "No Men," in the homes regulation, I reminded them. "You don't have to depend on a man to pay your rent now."

Plenty of water for bathing and laundry.
audreydewys.com

Life with a purpose

The purpose of Ruuska Village was more than provision of a home off the streets. Ruuska Village provided the opportunity to make life changes and the "No Men" regulation gave me an opportunity to introduce Biblical principles. I told them, "The Bible says, 'Thou shalt not commit adultery.'"

It might sound like a rather harsh rule at first, but the women would have to change their lives if they were to stay out of the cycle of desperation. Furthermore, their example would be a pattern for future generations of young Haitian women. I continually reminded them, "You cannot sin your way to prosperity." God had blessed them with a new home, better than they could ever have dreamed of. They must use this as a stepping-stone toward the beginning of a whole new way of life. The best way to thank God for this opportunity was to be a true Christian inside and out. I encouraged them to take pride in themselves, their new home, and live as an example of God's blessings to others. I tried to teach them to live with purpose rather than just living any old way they could to get by.

CHAPTER 5

More Than A Roof

Ruuska Village began with two houses and a supply depot. As funds came in, we added more homes for the single women and their children. The houses were made of block with a poured concrete floor, weather-worthy roof, vented blocks for windows and a secure locking steel entry door.

Although I had hauled in tons of fill, by the time the eleventh house was built we learned that the back of the lot would have to be elevated another three feet in order for water to flow to the front of the property where we could then pump it into the street. One year excessive rain drenched Haiti. Two feet of water covered the yard, but the houses – built on a higher level and on concrete slabs remained dry. With the use of sump pumps we were able to control the water.

Protection

As someone involved in the many aspects of construction and maintenance of homes, I understood the necessity of homes that provided protection of both property, possessions, and person. It seemed that every month brought new challenges to protecting and maintaining the village.

We walled in the Ruuska Village to protect the homes, keep the public from wandering throughout the houses and to keep marauding goats from eating the trees and garden plants. Few of the women had ever lived in a house with a door that locked. At night furniture had often barricaded flimsy doors. A steel locking door on each house gave the women a sense of both protection and a sense of control over the few possessions they had.

Having our own well enabled the women to do laundry, keep their homes and bodies clean, use flush toilets, and water their gardens. Since the well was 100 feet deep, we didn't worry too much about contamination. That all changed, though, when Joe Hurston, the founder and very active leader of *Air Mobile Ministries*, visited Ruuska Village.

In 2004, tropical storm Jeanne flooded the area of Gonaïves, killing 2500 people. Making matters worse, seriously contaminated water caused a rapid onset of waterborne diseases and took more lives. When Joe Hurston and a group of volunteers came to Haiti with Vortex Voyager TM water purifiers, I volunteered to provide transportation and accompany Joe and the group to Gonaïves. I met everyone at the airport in Port-au-Prince, loaded the truck with their baggage and off we went. We made a quick stop at Ruuska Village to pick up more supplies before heading to ground zero in Gonaïves. This was the first time Joe had visited Ruuska Village. The whole group enjoyed seeing the children and meeting the workers at the village.

During our time driving to Gonaïves Joe asked many questions about the village and the children. I gladly shared the story about how the village was only two years old and had been started to create a better life for mothers and their children.

"We drilled a well," I proudly told Joe. "We got sweet (not saline) water at 100 feet and now we are even able to provide water for others in the community."

"Do you buy bottled water for the babies?" he asked.

"We buy bottled water for the young babies and American volunteers that visit us, but the rest of us drink the well water."

"How much diarrhea medicine do you buy?" Joe asked."

"Lots!" I answered. "I give out diarrhea medicine almost every day. I can't keep it on hand, but you know Haiti."

"Barbara," Joe said "the Voyager could purify the well water and make it safe for everyone. Pure water would prevent so much diarrhea. You wouldn't have to buy water again."

I didn't doubt the value of the purifier, but buying one wasn't in our budget at the current time.

In Gonaïves, I watched as Joe showed people how to use the machine. The purifier could take murky contaminated ditch water and turn it into pure drinking water. I saw the light of hope on people's faces as they received pure water. This purifier was truly a gift from God to the people of Gonaïves.

We don't need it any more—diarrhea medicine.

Before the group went back to the USA, Joe presented Ruuska Village with one Voyager water purifier. Shortly thereafter the 60-100 people who lived in or visited Ruuska Village had pure water to drink all the time. On a set schedule, the children pumped water to be purified, and the women cleaned, sterilized and filled empty bottles with pure water.

One month after receiving the first unit, I was talking with a friend and I suddenly stopped and said, "I just realized that I'm not handing out diarrhea medicine anymore. No one at the village has diarrhea. What a shock!" A year later, we received a second purifier which enabled us to purify what we needed more quickly.

Another story that shows the powerful impact that the Voyager has had in our village involves a time when the unit wasn't available. I made a trip to Washington State to take some children to their new home. In the rush of preparation I locked the Voyager units in my office. One week later I received a frantic phone call from the village supervisor. They had run out of purified water and couldn't get access to the purifiers. Almost every adult and child in the village had diarrhea. After getting a key to the office, they were able to purify more water. Soon, everyone was healthy again, but the incident helped the women in the village recognize the value of pure clean water.

Power issues

Power was another essential and expensive utility for the development of Ruuska Village. After connecting to EDH (Electricity D' Haiti) we soon learned the utility was not a reliable source for electricity. We then turned to generators and eventually invertors to provide electricity for three buildings. When the small generator broke, Ruuska Village received generous donations from adoptive families which enabled the purchase of a good quality, large capacity generator that provided electricity to all the homes in the village.

The all-important "we"

The "we" that I refer to was an expanding group of supporters and volunteers who came to pour concrete, lay block, and conduct children's programs (adults enjoyed too). I never could have built and sustained Ruuska Village without volunteers.

Caring for the volunteers, though, provided a different set of challenges which necessitated building basic accommodations for them. Volunteers don't ask for much but if you provide three essentials they will return and encourage friends to volunteer. Volunteers need: safe water and food, a means of cleaning up after working in the tropical heat, and a good night's rest. Since our acreage was limited, expansion had to go upward, so we added a second story on Number 2 House to provide a kitchen and bath for visitors.

Volunteers not only came to work and lighten our load, they came with low-cost ideas to improve Ruuska Village. One Florida church sent groups to develop a play yard for the children. They painted Noah's Ark decorations on the houses and made time to play with the children. Later, a covered play room provided both shelter for the children during the rainy season, and a place for choir practice and Bible studies.

Through the years, we not only maintained and built more buildings, but brought improvement to the homes. Concrete floors were tiled and security bars installed on windows. Our growth, however, was not all for the benefit of the village. A clothing depot and food depot served both the needs of the village women and hundreds of people in the community.

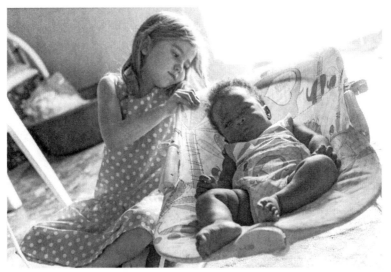

Visitors and volunteers always stay busy in Ruuska Village. While Audrey deWys photo-documents the work of Reach Out to Haiti, her daughter rocks one of the babies.
Photography by audreydewys.com

Adding a clinic

From the beginning of Reach Out to Haiti, I tried to help people get medical care. That could mean anything from handing out aspirin to transporting people to a hospital. Often doctors and nurses came and volunteered to treat village families and surrounding neighbors but we had no facility from which they could work. Furthermore, the medical costs of taking children to clinics in preparation for adoption was increasing the financial burden on the adoption agency.

The Ewing family in South Carolina recognized the need for a clinic and volunteered to raise the necessary funds. Through generous donations, we were soon able to build the Aaron Ewing medical clinic at the village. Continued donations kept the clinic stocked with 99% of all the medical supplies needed for the village people and hundreds of people living outside of the village.

First clinic patient

Before we officially opened the Aaron Ewing Memorial Clinic at Ruuska Village, Dr. Aaron and Thereasa Clark from Michigan came down to visit their "soon to be adopted son" Stephen Felix. Stephen was celebrating his first birthday, and the proud "soon-to-be" parents came to celebrate with him. I hoped that during their stay Dr. Clark would help me set up the new clinic. The job would involve moving mountains of medical supplies and medications from the main depot to the clinic building. We also had to sort, label, and inventory supplies and dispose of all outdated or useless items.

I took little Stephen with me on the one-hour trip to the airport and two-hour wait for the plane in the air-conditioned truck. On the way back to the village, Stephen began to cough. We assumed the air-conditioning was causing his coughing.

During the night, though, his symptoms grew worse. He developed a fever and difficulty breathing. Having a doctor for a father sure came in handy. Dr. Clark diagnosed Stephen's problem as pneumonia. Little Stephen became the first patient at the clinic.

Our panicked search in the middle of the night, for the right medications and a breathing machine, showed how important it was to set up the clinic supply room. Stephen's medical condition was critical and he required breathing treatments four to six times a day. Dr. Clark extended his visit for four extra days until his son's health was stable. During that time, we got all the supplies moved, cataloged and Dr. Clark was able to treat many more sick people.

Our God knows of all our needs long before they manifest themselves. Through the dedicated fund raising efforts of the Ewings, donations to the building fund, donated medical supplies and medicine— and a breathing machine that the Clarks had donated the year before— Stephen's life was spared. God's plan was set in motion over two years before to save this one precious life. We praise God that all of us were used as part of this wonderful miracle.

CHAPTER 6

Window of Being

As the village started to become a family group, the women started to help each other and for the most part observed the rules of the village. As a reward, I helped each woman obtain her birth certificate, ID card and a passport.

Identity

Few even had a birth certificate. Obtaining these documents for each woman was expensive, but it proved to be one of the best things I ever did for them. The women suddenly had a documented identity. They became an "official" person which gave them self-esteem.

Problems arose, though, when trying to determine their family and heritage. We had to search for family members who knew where the ladies were born and the names of their mothers and fathers. Yes, many of them did not even know the names of their family members. In order to come to a reasonable birthdate we asked family members questions such as: Do you know when Christa was born? Who was the president? Was it rainy season? How does she place with the births of her siblings? Was she 1, 2,

3, 4, etc.? Then, combined with other information, we decided on a birthdate and obtained a birth certificate. The process often took months. Next I helped them apply for ID cards, electoral cards, and finally passports.

Wow! What a change. With documents in hand that established their personhood, they started acting differently. Fights over dress rules ended. No more naked ladies bathing in the yard and children even wore panties. Abilities and talents began to develop in the ladies. Some were better mothers than others. Others learned to sew, do hair or do manicures. Several of the women had "green thumbs" and enjoyed caring for the trees and plants that provided additional food and shade for the village. Some even had the gift of teaching. Many were hard, dedicated workers and others were not so ambitious. As a family group, though, they began to share work and help each other.

The depression that plagued so many of the women faded away and they began to show pride in being part of a higher class of people than being a street person. With an identity, they could get a real job, they could attend good schools and they could even get an electoral card and vote in the elections. They were "somebody."

The women began to show their gratefulness to Reach Out to Haiti ministry and all the people that financially supported Ruuska Village. They showed their gratefulness by living as a loving family, helping and being helped by each other and by submitting to all the village rules. They showed it in the way they respected themselves and each other, and by loving and caring for all the children as if they were their own.

I also live at Ruuska Village and know that life here is not perfect, but I also know that the quality of life for the women and children is way above the life they had before coming to the village.

As the support base for Reach Out to Haiti grew, Ruuska Village grew. Cargos of food and supplies began to fill the depots and the ladies started to receive a weekly food allotment. The allotment was not enough to supply all their needs, just enough to help and encourage them, because I wanted the women to learn to take the initiative to work. Thus, the women had to work in the village to provide for the rest of their own children's needs. I also provided the formula, diapers, food and clothing for the children who were in the process of being adopted.

CHAPTER 7

Shoddy Building Materials

The work of Reach Out to Haiti and the Ruuska Village spreads far beyond giving a single mother shelter or finding a loving family for a child. It's almost impossible to work in Haiti and focus on one need only. Haiti's problems are linked to each other. If you deal with one problem, you soon find yourself involved in a linking problem. One area that links to almost every problem in Haiti is lack of education.

I have done legal paperwork on hundreds of adoptions over the years here in Haiti. Naturally, the families of these children are poor and generally poorly educated or self-educated. Many of the parents or relatives are unable to even sign their names on the relinquishment papers; they simply place an X and a fingerprint on the paperwork as a form of identification. I question them about their education. Did you attend school? How many years? I found that many who attended school for five or six years were unable to sign their name or read.

Most of the women in Ruuska Village could not read or write. One visitor sat with the women one at a time to teach them how to write their names. All but two learned this skill. I started having them sign for their pay so they could practice.

Financial burden

In Haiti nearly all schools have specific uniforms and dress codes. This means that even if you pay the tuition to attend the school, if you are unable to wear proper shoes, purchase the required uniform, wear the correct colored socks and/or ribbons, you will be sent home and will not be allowed to attend class until all required dress codes have been met. School expenses are a tremendous financial burden on most families.

So consider this: picture a poor family, barely managing to feed their children, suffering from the perils of unemployment and lack of decent medical care, and many times living with friends or family members because they can't afford rent for their own shack. They have several children and want desperately to put them in school so that they will be able to get a decent job and have a better future. So the search for the money begins. They may go to relatives, they may contact family in the US to help with the tuition expenses, or they may get money or sponsorship from churches or missionary organizations. The amount of extra funds they find will determine if, or how many, children will go to school.

Lack of texts and supplies

Most schools do not supply pencils, paper, text books or other supplies that might be necessary. The size of the classroom varies greatly, but usually, a room will have four to eight different grades, separated only by large standing chalkboards. Since few students can afford textbooks, lessons are taught by writing them on the chalkboard and having the children recite the lesson. As with most kids, some get it and some don't. The children who know the lessons will proudly scream it at the top of their voice to let the teacher know how smart they are and the others will generally sit quietly and uncomprehending as the next lesson is begun.

Lack of verifiable credentials and accreditation.

By Haitian law, instructors are required to have attended school, completed (or at least have paid for) the assigned number of class years (which may or may not correspond to the *actual* number of years) and pass the government exam before they are allowed to teach. *Again*, this is not generally enforced. Almost anyone can make false papers or pay for a passing grade. Few places bother to check a teacher's credentials.

Schools are started by all types of people. Churches use their buildings for school during the week days. Mission organizations open many schools. Sadly, some who own or rent a large building and want to make easy money will paint cartoon pictures on one of the concrete walls, make up an officially sounding title, hire a (sometimes) educated person for next to nothing to teach, and then begin collecting tuition from unsuspecting, uneducated parents who want a better life for their children.

Language barriers

French is the *official* language of Haiti, and many classes are taught in French. Most children, especially among the poor have heard only Creole. The children go from Creole (spoken language) to French (legal language) and embark on learning a new language for every part of school. Just think about it, they might just as well be dropped into a foreign country with no dictionary.

With no textbooks, lessons are learned by rote, and the children memorize answers to questions they do not understand. For example, when asked in French to define *science*, the child will recite the correct answer in French. When asked in Creole to define *science*, the child has no idea of what science is and no understanding of what the memorized question or answer means.

On the pro side, since French is the official national language, the successful student would be more apt to fit into a higher class socially and would better be able to advance in continuing education. More education means more employability and even an opportunity to work in government jobs given only to French-educated people. For a Haitian student, though, learning a new language is not optional, it is necessary to have a chance of success in life.

Cultural biases

So October comes around and, if all has gone well, the family may be able to send the **oldest boy** to school and, maybe, if things have gone very well, they have enough to send one girl to school. So far, this scenario is sad but to be expected in Haiti. When school starts, though, cultural biases kick in. I have personally observed this practice over and over again and I am convinced that this must be numbered among the greatest problems with Haitian culture. Again, picture the family that is fortunate enough to have a boy and a girl going to school. The boy rises in the morning and the mother will bathe and dress him, fix him breakfast and off to school he goes. He is special; he is a **"student."** His only job now is to study and play soccer. Often that special standing as "student" turns into pride that grows quickly into lazy arrogance. Male "students" do no work, they carry no water, they help no one and expect to be served, allowed to study and play soccer. That is all that anyone expects of them.

On the other hand, the girl rises in the morning, washes, dresses, attends school. After classes she cleans, cooks, carries water, gathers charcoal, runs errands as needed, babysits the younger children, and serves her elders. If she is lucky, she works rather quickly, and may have time for study.

47

Meanwhile, the boy attends school year after year, plays soccer, does no work and is treated like royalty in the home. Often, a young man will proudly grow a very long fingernail on his pinky to show everyone that he is a student and does *no manual labor.*

Exemption, not preparation

So the years pass and the male "student" is now 22 or 23 years old and has finally finished high school. He hasn't done a single day's manual work during the entire time as a student. The very *word* work is foreign to him and, of course, now that he is an **educated man**—he has status. With **education,** he must choose a job befitting of his class, such as a business position or government job. Tragically, without a strong middle class in Haiti, the young man is left trying to make the long leap to "upper class" work.

Disillusionment and results

The stigma of manual labor is imbedded in Haitian culture and prevents many men from taking jobs that would provide income and stability for their families. Decent-paying manual job openings are few and far between in Haiti and non-manual jobs are even more scarce.

Unless a young man has special friends with influence he has little chance of finding satisfactory employment. With the right connections he might find employment, but it is not likely. Now, this nearly grown man has nothing to do. Most likely he will spend his days with other discontented and disillusioned young men who are now **educated** but unemployed. They quickly become arrogant, angry and resentful. They congregate and discuss their mistreatment by government and society and soon start riots, manifestations, protests, and political demonstrations, that escalate into violence. The ensuing destruction, fires and anarchy further contribute to the lack of employment opportunities.

Education that provides income

In spite of the problems of education and limited employment opportunities, I still encourage education. Reach Out to Haiti spends thousands of dollars helping children go to school every year.

Some of the mothers in Ruuska Village choose to send their children to preschools and schools outside of the village and we provide financial help to cover the tuition, books and uniform costs. Because of the danger and violence that plagues Haiti, though, I felt that the children being adopted were safer attending school in the village, so we established a daily preschool for the 10 to 15 children who do not attend regular school.

We encourage the women of Ruuska Village to continue their education, Some of the women attend grade school, but we also help them get assistance and training for realistic employment. Being a nanny, a nail tech, or housekeeper may not make them wealthy, but the work will provide the necessities for their families.

Adult education

One of our best adult educational programs is our **child-care program**. Many of the children awaiting adoption live in one of our child-care homes. I pay a family to care for children in their homes. I find that the children receive better care, more affection, more physical and mental stimulation, more one on one attention, and the start of what a "family" will be like in their new homes, which in many cases is severely lacking from where they have come. I provide the food, clothing, health care products, etc., that the child needs and pay the caregiver a salary while they care for their own children, as well. In this way both the child and the family benefit from the program.

Small business packages.

We also have the ability, through donations, to provide a large suitcase full of clothes, shoes, linens, toys, etc. to people that need a little more help. These suitcases are given to families that need money for rent, school payments, medical needs, or just food. Recipients are encouraged to sell the items to obtain the money they need. This is work, not a handout of goods or money. They can come in every six months for this package. Rent is due every six months so, hopefully, this money will keep a roof over their heads. I am not a believer in giving out money. I believe they should do a job of some kind to obtain the money they need. My goal is to give a bit of food and a bit of help to encourage them to provide for their family's needs.

Job training

I pay for enrollment for each of the women in the Muci Sales School and when they complete the course they get $350 to start a small business. Some of the women receive job offers and some sell goods in the street.

LOCATION, LOCATION, LOCATION

CHAPTER 8

"Why Do You Stay?"

Life in Haiti is very difficult. I can leave any time I want, but the Haitians can't.

"Why do you stay in Haiti?" some ask. "Why do you keep working so hard at this?"

I jokingly say, "Because it never gets boring."

People guess at my reasons. They say, "You must love Haiti," or "You just love the children." Some people say, "You must like the weather." As I was preparing to fly back to Haiti one day, my sister came up with the best reason for returning to Haiti.

She said, "We three sisters are crusaders like our mother and father. We fight to lift up the discouraged and poor. We try to build them up and help them improve their lives." She pointed out that the three of us work with poor underprivileged people. My younger sister works in an ESL (English as a Second Language) program in Upper State New York. My older sister runs a feeding program for the poor in Florida. Me, I fight my way through government bureaucracies to give children a better life and guide women to a better living standard.

To me, my work is more than serving the poor and underprivileged. I believe God has sent me to do this work which gives urgency to include Biblical teachings in my work. My ultimate goal is to end Voodoo and teach God's plan of salvation to everyone. My realistic goal is to reach as many people as possible. I purchase Bibles and tracts. I can't keep them in supply. Everyone is anxious to hear about Jesus. I'm not a pastor, Bible scholar or prophet. I'm just a child of God trying to share the blessings and peace God has given me with the people of Haiti.

My days are not spent in a rocking chair in Ruuska Village overseeing the women. I travel to the city almost every day. My assistance to the needy does not stop when I exit Ruuska Village. My truck looks like a combination cargo truck and Haitian tap-tap.

If you saw me on the street you would say, "There goes a 'bag lady.'" I carry Tylenol, cough meds, first aid supplies, vitamins, layettes, Bibles, tracts, clothing, health and hygiene supplies, adoption records, photos of adopted children, candy, toys, formula and so much more. When it is hot and dry in Haiti the air is dusty and full of pollution. Allergies, respiratory problems, and fevers plague the poor and the old. I do what I can to alleviate the symptoms.

Few poor women have pre-natal care. Through donations from several people we have been able to provide vitamins, some lab tests and at least one visit to a doctor. When we see poor, obviously pregnant women on the street we often stop and give them pre-natal vitamins and as we have funds we pay a midwife or clinic to aid in delivery. We welcome the new baby into this world with a nice new layette. Too many mothers and sometimes babies die during delivery or shortly after. We hope the help we provide makes a little difference.

You have to have a sense of humor

During the first year of living in a foreign environment, everything is novel and interesting. By the end of the second year, the novelty has worn thin and you find yourself mentally making changes to what you feel is wrong in the culture. Since you really can't make those changes and have to accept them, frustration, anger and resentment set in UNLESS you deal with the culture with a good dose of humor. I'm afraid my humor is often tinted with sarcasm, so if you feel that everything in a culture is sacred and should only be dealt with in a serious and **always** respectful manner, you may want to skip reading LOCATION, LOCATION, LOCATION.

Just exit for Rest Areas

In Haiti, we often get caught in delays with bumper to bumper traffic that goes nowhere. On one such occasion, Joe Hurston was driving his van with Cindy in the front seat and I was with children in the back seat. Traffic had not moved for 40 minutes. But fear not, we can always find some unusual thing to amuse us as we wait. This day, we watched the man in the car in front of us. He drove a Honda Civic, the one with a paper holder on the door, recessed handles and lots of pockets on the door.

The man was as annoyed as we were that the traffic was not moving, but Joe commented about how the man seemed unusually distressed and was wiggling around in the seat. We soon saw why. He opened the car door, got out, and facing the car door and his back to us, he unzipped his pants and began to pee.

Joe quietly said to Cindy and me, "Do you see that?"

"I see it," I said.

When the man finally finished, he did his little shake, sat down in the car and slammed the door shut. Instantly, he threw open the door and with face dripping, he looked furiously for the person who dared throw water in his face.

We laughed until we could hardly catch our breath. He had peed into all the pockets and recessed handles as well as the paper holder at the bottom of the door. When he slammed the door, he had a showered himself with his own pee.

Why pay??

Are you old enough to remember the Edsel car? This was a product of the Ford Motor Company. This car was produced near the end of the fifties and was given the name of Henry Ford's son. Henry Ford was famous for his good business sense, but this car was an automotive failure. The Edsel was probably the biggest goof in the automotive industry. I'm sure each of us can name a product or service that failed. Some products reach the public at the wrong time. Had they been introduced earlier or later they might have been a great success.

From time to time, Haiti goes through spurts of economic change. Enterprises such as pizza places, cyber cafes, ice factories and water purifying facilities have done well. Street vendors who sell water, popsicles and ice cream bars, and gas stations that stock fast food and groceries have also succeed. Some people have shown good business sense by accurately predicting the demands of the country **and** what the people will pay for or buy.

One particular business, however, ended up being as successful as the Edsel. There was, indeed, a need for their business, but the entrepreneurs had definitely not researched the people's **desire** for their service or the necessity of maintaining the business.

Anyone who has been to Haiti or knows anything about third world countries, can tell you that there are few designated toilet facilities. Ladies in skirts and dresses gracefully squat along public streets and men stop, turn their back to traffic and pee against a wall. This way of relieving oneself is socially acceptable. Court houses, public buildings, small business offices, churches and parks reek of a strong smell of urine.

In the year of 2000, we noticed blue port-a-pots near the airport, post office, and several other public areas. After a curious examination, we discovered they were pay toilets. Yes, believe it or not, Haiti had a new business... PAY TOILETS!!! The cost was two gourdes and a three minute limit was posted on each sign.

When I passed the port-a-pots I watched to see if anyone entered, but all I ever saw were men peeing outside, alongside the booths. One day, when I was shopping near the post office, a young lady with me said, "I need to find a toilet."

"Let's go to the pay toilet," I suggested. We found a man accepting the money and I asked about the three-minute limit. He said we could take all the time we needed.

Whew! I would like to see the person who could handle being in the toilet **three minutes**. Apparently emptying the port-a-pots was not part of the business. The few people who would "pay to pee" would never return to the stench. There was no hope for success on this venture. This business was doomed for failure.

Adjustable Ages

When I'm asked if I will ever get married again, I jokingly say, "Oh yes, I'm looking for just the right man. I'm looking for him in the coronary intensive care units of the hospital?" Or maybe I told you that if I could find a BLUE man I would get married. Too many people said if I married him he would soon be blue. Let me set you straight. I mean the color blue not his personality. As they say... time will tell, and I do think I finally found a good reason to get married.

One day a lady came to my office and recognized Johny, the young man that works for me.

"Your father was a pastor in Montrouis?" she asked.

"Yes," Johny answered.

"Pastor Antoine is such a wonderful man," she said. "My husband was much older than me, and I was too young to marry but he married us." She could not say enough good things about the pastor because he had helped her and her husband bypass a Haitian law. (In Haiti, you must be 18 years old and the man and lady must be close in age to marry.)

"No problem," as they say in Haiti. The pastor had "given" her some of the man's years, and married them. Do you get the point? If the man gives her ten years she is over 18 and he is closer to her age. I checked this out and it is indeed a common practice in Haiti. I quickly realized why the birth certificate ages and the marriage certificate ages never match. I thought the pastor was just guessing or they couldn't remember their ages.

So, getting back to plans for my "blessed event." I decided I would give some young man 15 of my years and get married. How can I lose? I'll be 15 years younger. Fifteen years ago I could see better, hear better and was 50 lbs. lighter. What a deal! Just thinking about it makes me feel younger already.

I have a lot to offer a young Haitian man. Fifteen years of knowledge and a **USA RESIDENT VISA**. I'll surely have my pick… they will line up for the opportunity. I'll let you know the wedding date when I finish preparing the pre-nuptial agreement. Oh, yes, we will definitely have a pre-nuptial agreement

Driver's test

Driving in Haiti is not for the timid or slow-to-react drivers. Consider first that most people in Haiti just buy a driver's license. There are driving schools and tests, but in the long run, it is cheaper and easier to just buy a driver's license. One popular way is to make a counterfeit USA license then trade it in for a Haiti license. Others pay to have a Haitian license made. I don't know of anyone who actually took classes and a government driver's test. When driving in Haiti, remember, you may be the only truly licensed driver on the road.

All drives are scenic

Broken-down vehicles are everywhere. If it breaks down in the middle of the road, leave it there until you can repair it. "Broken-down" could mean a flat tire, a drive shaft that needs replacing, or even a three-day motor job. You put some green tree branches on the road behind the vehicle and leave it there until it is repaired. Since there are no lights on broken-down vehicles, driving at night on country highways is discouraged. Many travelers have been killed by driving into and under heavily loaded trucks that blocked a lane.

In the city, you have to watch out for "car catchers." No, these aren't thieves. They are drains or man holes without covers. You seldom notice them until a wheel drops into one with a teeth-jarring clunk. Fear not! Two to four men will be standing close by to lift your car from the hole—for a fee. They are probably the same men that took the cover from the hole and sold it for scrap metal.

The roads are in such poor condition that only one side of the road is often passable. You have to drive in and around potholes and obstacles continuously. Rocks and rubble, broken glass, pieces of metal, and stalled vehicles force drivers to take a meandering path onto any available lane, sidewalk or roadside path. Flat tires are so common that little repair stands appear at intersections and quarter-mile intervals. Having dependable transportation requires ownership of more than one vehicle because one is always being repaired.

Most of the roads have two lanes, but handle five lanes of traffic. Pulling out into city traffic requires, sticking the front bumper into the lane, then edging the car out forcing the traffic to swerve around you. Space allowance between vehicles is not measured by feet, but by hand-width. Some cars have rubber hands sticking out the sides of the car to let you know you are too close to another car. Side mirrors often thwack pedestrians and sometimes donkeys. It is somewhat like driving using the Braille system.

Surprisingly, most fatal traffic accidents involve fast buses and large over-loaded trucks, which are driven fast and recklessly. When the UN entered the country they brought in many cars and increased traffic. UN drivers showed little respect to other drivers and caused many accidents.

We do have driving laws in Haiti, but most drivers haven't a clue what they are. No one stops at stop signs. No one takes a traffic light seriously. Police officers sometime check for registration and a driver license. Near the holidays the stops seem to increase and people are hassled over minor offenses such as not using a seat belt. These overly eager-to-enforce driving laws officers are usually very considerate. They will allow you to pay the fine (only cash) **to them** which will keep you from having to go to court. If you drive away, saying that you will pay it in court, they will usually call you back and offer to reduce the fine **if** you **pay them** on the spot (in cash). One American drove away four times before he got the officer to reduce the fine to a reasonable amount (in cash).

If they really want to give you a hard time, they will take your license and send you away. Then, you must retrieve the license from a police station later. That can be a bit difficult, because you're not always told which station to go to. It is much easier to give them your USA license. You can purchase a new one in the US for $15. If you give your Haiti license to them, you must pay more money to get it back, that is, if you can find who has it. Years ago, I would give them any photo ID, like a BJ's card, and since many could not read they would nod acceptance and let me go. After the US trained the traffic police, though, that trick didn't work.

A *"good"* man

Philomene had 12 siblings from her father. Her father was considered a "good" man because he had so many children. It did not matter how many women he had babies with or if he actually raised the children. Yes, just the fact that he was the biological father to many children made him a "good" man in the eyes of Haitians.

Part of the culture in Haiti values a person by how many children they have. Children are considered gifts from God. Some also take a fatalistic attitude believing that certain health related conditions, including pregnancy, are determined only by God. The polygamist lifestyle of many Haitian men further contributes to having many children. Those who have a decent income may maintain more than one household. Unemployed men or those with extremely low income, however, often abandon families and go on to start another relationship.

Women hold similar views about having many children. It doesn't matter if the children starve to death, are sent to an orphanage, placed for adoption, abandoned, neglected, or abused. She is a "good" mother if she has had many children, no matter who is the father. This is what happens when accepted cultural behavior is contrary to the laws of the Bible. Haiti is plagued by cultural beliefs that defy family and relationship guidelines in the Bible.

CHAPTER 9

Death Isn't Always A Permanent Condition

All Saints Day

In the United States we celebrate October 31st as Halloween. In Haiti, a country where Voodoo is the oldest religion, they celebrate this as All Hallows, All Saints Day or the Day of the Dead. Haitians celebrating All Hallows visit cemeteries to pay respects to the dead in a two-day national holiday that offers food, alcohol and flowers to Baron Samdi, the guardian of the dead in Voodoo.

One night, when Johny and I had worked late and traveled home after dark we noticed the Bon Repos cemetery was lit up like a Christmas tree. People were bringing food and gifts and lighting candles at the large black cross that represented Baron Samdi.

The next morning, when we drove past the cemetery we saw an enormous black pig devouring gifts that adorned the large black cross. He even stepped up on another monument in order to get to a vegetable that hung from the cross. That pig ate enough fruits and vegetables to feed a family for a week. They say that nobody sees the baron during the daytime—maybe he does appear, but disguised as a pig.

Funerals and processions

Haitians honor the dead with large expensive funerals. The size and community participation in the funeral reflects the importance of the person. Tragically, the dead person may have been destitute and unable to pay for antibiotics or other medicine that could have saved their life.

So, the person dies. The family must then beg, borrow, or even steal to get the thousands of dollars for an elaborate funeral. After all, they want their loved one to be remembered as a good person. Sometimes, the body is placed in a cold storage vault until the family can raise money for a funeral and the relatives and friends that live outside Haiti can come for the funeral.

In some countries, the mourners wear black clothing, but in Haiti the funeral dress is usually white. The funeral will have flower arrangements, music, and hundreds of mourners that walk as far as a mile from the church to the gravesite. Mourners will include friends, relatives, professional mourners, musicians, and a videographer to record the procession.

Well-to-do families have a family crypt. If a family doesn't have a crypt they rent a space in someone's crypt. In the cemetery, the casket is placed in an opening in a very large concrete house-type building. The top is decorated with artistic concrete and steel figures. The opening will usually have an iron gate that can be locked and an altar-type shelf inside where candles, religious statues, a cross, flowers, family photos, cigarettes, or rum can be placed. Along with Voodoo symbols, the grave site may be strewn with fruits, vegetables and gifts to ensure a blessing on the dead. Christian graves, though, do not have Voodoo symbols or offerings.

The casket is cemented into the crypt with iron bars, so that the body cannot escape. One of the greatest fears of a family is that the body will return as a zombie. In Haiti, the fear of zombies is real. Unlike the amusing horror movies we watch, Haitians fear the walking dead and they make extra efforts to seal the grave with bars and cement so the body cannot escape.

How does one become a zombie and escape the grave? Some explain it this way. Some person may hate another man, covet his land, envy his wealth or maybe even his wife. So he may go to the witch doctor and purchase a potion. This poison is extracted from the glands of the blow fish and a small amount of the toxic poison will put a person into a coma. The person has not died, but the metabolism, heart rate, and breathing seem nonexistent. The person is mistakenly pronounced dead and buried alive.

Now the evil one who did this terrible deed may choose to return to the grave and release the person. By this time, though, the person has suffered severe brain damage from a lack of oxygen in the coffin. Sometimes the buried person will remember who they are and attempt to return home. **This does not work out well**. The family is terrified of the walking dead, and believe the person has become an evil zombie. After all, they **know** they buried this **dead** person. The victim will be feared and rejected by all.

Where then does this person go? The person cannot live long without food and water. Due to brain damage, the person cannot care for himself, so the only hope is to be a servant of the evil person who did this to him.

Grave rental

When I show American visitors around Port-au-Prince I often take them to the big cemetery. We walk around looking at the crypts and I always stop to point out the ones that have a big red X on them. The red X means that the crypts will be demolished if the family does not take better care of them. The same red X might also mean the crypt rent is in arrears.

While conducting one tour of the city, I noticed that the cemetery gates were locked. As I did a U-turn to leave I couldn't believe my own eyes. "Look! Look!" I exclaimed. Heaps of smashed coffins lay just inside the gates and along the street outside the cemetery.

This seemed unusual even in Haiti, but I soon forgot about the sight. A couple of days later Johny and I were waiting at the Contributions office when a man approached us selling a small French newspaper. I bought one and Johnny started reading it. Suddenly he started chuckling. Since I couldn't read French, he translated an article titled, "It's a Joke."

> *We, the members of the **association of the old dead people** in the big cemetery of Port-au-Prince, are screaming, "Help!" The thieves are making big money. They are stealing the hardware from our coffins and the gold from our teeth. They steal our crowns of eternity and make our homes forts full of guns. They are destroying our rest and eternal peace. They make our life and death not count. They invade our homes at midnight. The association would like the living people to know that today is life and tomorrow is death. It they don't do something to protect us one day we will take our complaints to the streets!"*

Me. Baron/President and Gran Baroness/Secretary

Keeping up with lies

On August 5, 1998, a sixteen-year-old girl gave birth to a beautiful baby girl. Unable to care for the baby, the mother came to me desperate to give "Baby Love" away. A lawyer, however, said I couldn't place her for adoption because the mother was only sixteen. I still paid for the birth certificate, did a social study, lab tests, doctor exam, photo, and gave the mother clothes and food. I continued to help the Mom until she stopped coming. About seven months later Mom returned to tell me the baby had died.

She seemed very sad. All I could do was give her the photos I had taken and express how sorry I was that the baby had died. A year later, she returned, pregnant again and worried about the unborn baby not moving. I took her to the doctor and an ultrasound showed the baby was doing fine. She was also told this child would be a boy. Just before the birth of the baby boy, Mom came to see me with an emergency. She told me this story.

When Baby Love was six months old, Mom had taken her to Mirebalais and asked a friend to care for her while she went to the Dominican Republic. When she returned the friend told her that the baby had died. That was when she had come to tell me the baby had died. Recently, Mom had gone to visit her friend in Mirebalais and found the baby alive and well and named Rose China.

Angry, Mom had gone to a judge who ruled that she could have the baby back but had to pay the friend for childcare. Mom hopped on a bus immediately and came right to my office.

"You must take this baby right now!" she insisted. "I can't take her home. I told everyone she was dead. I'm going to have a new baby now. I can't feed two babies."

Mom was now old enough to get an ID card and legally give up her child for adoption, so after the legal aspects were sorted out, Rose China was adopted by a family in Ohio. Death is not always a permanent condition in Haiti, but Rose China was the first baby I had that came back to life.

Often, years after an adoption is complete, possibly ten or even sixteen years later, the dead parents or single dead mothers show up asking for news and photos of their child. I give both parents and children any information that I have. The child needs to know that the parents are alive so I take a photo of the parent or parents holding death certificates. I explain to the children that I would not adopt out a child who had a mother or father who could care for them. The parents could not care for the child so they had purchased a death certificate so that the child could have a good life in another safe country.

CHAPTER 10

Landscape

As different situations developed in the country, I watched with curiosity and often head-shaking amazement at how the people responded.

Unique celebration

How do you celebrate the inauguration of a newly elected US president? Maybe you have been among the few that actually participated in the ceremonies, or you have stood on the streets of Washington D.C. to observe the festivities. Some watch the event on television, but most Americans switch the channel to a movie or sitcom.

Jean Bertrand Aristide was elected President in 1991 and 2000. I was in Haiti during the first election time and the country was plagued with fear, violence, and general unrest. When Aristide was inaugurated in 1992, the people celebrated and honored the new president. Roads were blocked to control and reduce violent demonstrations, but the celebrations took an unusual turn. People throughout Haiti put their tables, chairs, beds, and any other household items that they happened to have into the streets. To this day, I have no idea of "why" and I haven't been able to find a reason for this strange manner of celebration.

Aristide's first "victory" was filled with controversy and he was in exile for the majority of his term. In November of 2000, Aristide again ran, and was again "elected." Truly fair and honest elections are non-existent in Haiti.

As usual, when dealing with anything political in Haiti, violent demonstrations were predicted for inauguration day on February 7, 2001. I decided to distance myself from Port-au-Prince and traveled to Cap-Haïtien to visit friends, and check up on some children. I kept my eyes open for signs of demonstrations, but much to my surprise, there were no noticeable outbreaks of violence or public demonstrations along the road. My comment to my traveling companions was, "There's a first time for everything!"

In the afternoon, we ventured out into a peaceful Cap-Haïtien. "Can you believe this?" I said, as we began walking through the streets of O' Cap. Everywhere, tables, chairs, beds, and household goods had been hauled out to decorate the city. Street after street had colorful sheet-tents around beds decorated with satin bed linens. Tables spread with lace cloths held knick-knacks and vases filled with flowers. Bright paper chains and decorations, and banners streamed from light poles and the Haitian flag appeared everywhere. People had dragged their TVs and radios outside and everyone was watching and listening to the inaugural ceremony.

Their unusual way of celebrating the inauguration astonished me. I took so many photos that I ran out of film. I have asked everyday people, lawyers, pastors, doctors, psychologists, and social workers, but no one can give me a reason for this strange new custom. The people of Haiti did not do this before Aristide, they did not do it for the inauguration of President Preval during the years in between Aristide's terms, but they did it again for Aristide.

Neverland

Remember the story of Peter Pan, who lived in Neverland and never grew up? In 1998 the people of Haiti joined Peter Pan in Neverland from June 10th through July 13th.

No matter how desperate their lives, Haitians have the ability to find joy in one activity – soccer. During the World Cup Soccer games in 1998, Haiti overflowed with happy, fun-loving people. Those days weren't like the chaotic drunken celebration of good and evil prevalent during Mardi Gras. Anger, grudges, and resentments were forgotten during the World Cup as people gathered around radios and televisions to cheer for their favorite teams.

Without a doubt Brazil was the all-time favorite with Argentina the second favored team. People strung banners in streets, decorated tap taps and put flags on cars. They even wore uniforms of their favorite team. They lounged around radios in stores and clustered in front of windows that displayed the games on television. Screams of encouragement or moans of despair came from the fans and when a goal was made deafening cheers sounded. When a favorite team won people screamed and yelled, danced in the streets, patted each other on the back, and waved flags. Early evening trips home were often delayed due to spirited spur of the moment street parades. For one glorious month the people forgot the harsh realities of their lives and lived in a land of childlike glee and happiness.

The *Haitian Water Theory*

Half the life of Haitian children and women is spent getting water. Sometimes it means hiking up and down rocky mountain trails with gallon plastic jugs or 5-gallon buckets on their heads. In the city it means fighting for a place at a spigot where water is flowing.

During the UN occupation of Haiti, US soldiers developed a plan to bring water to people on Gonaïves. First they repaired the cistern that served as a reservoir, then ran a line of PVC pipe down the mountain. They put taps every few hundred yards so that people could draw water without having to walk up and down the mountain for it.

When the Special Forces designed the water plan for Gonaïves, however, they did not realize that the *Haitian Water Theory* regulated water resources. According to the *Haitian Water Theory:*

1. When water is available, get all that you can because it may not be there tomorrow. Flowing water must be **captured** today to prevent it from leaving.
2. I do not need to share water with my neighbor. **It's every person for self.**
3. Uncaptured water will either go to a neighbor (which I may not like) or drop off the mountain and be lost in the sea.

To guarantee a personal ongoing water supply, people drove spikes into the PVC where it passed their hut. Then they stuck a length of hose or a piece of bamboo in the hole and channeled the water into buckets. After their buckets had filled, they patched the hole with sticks, grass or rocks to prevent it from going past their house. The force of the water would loosen the debris but every few days the lines would clog and stop due to so much trash in the water line. After repairing and clearing the lines several times, the Special Forces abandoned the pipeline. Everyone went back to carrying water up and down the mountain in heavy containers.

The *Haitian Water Theory* also regulates city fountains. One fountain ran day and night, wasting water, so Special Forces installed a faucet so the water could be turned on and off. As in the mountains the spigot fell under the authority of the *Haitian Water Theory* and the "every man for himself," policy kicked in.

71

One industrious individual decided that if he took the handle from the spigot he could have his own personal key and instant access to all the water he wanted **when** he wanted it. The next person who came for water felt that the water should be shared. His solution was to take a rock and smash the whole nozzle. Result? The water ran all the time again.

The hardest work

Some men in Haiti feel that manual labor is beneath them. Others work very, very hard. With an unemployment rate over 40% most available jobs require hard physical labor such as cleaning streets or shoveling dirt or rock for construction projects. The hardest work in Haiti is pulling a *brouette*, a two-wheeled conveyance often loaded with hundreds of pounds of sugar cane or raw, blood-oozing hides. Pulling a *brouette* loaded with nearly a ton of cargo strains every muscle, bone and organ in the body and is said to reduce the laborer's life expectancy to about 35 years. Recently a recycling business began in Haiti, which has provided additional demand for *brouette* laborers.

In Haiti, an item that goes to a recycling facility, truly has no further use. With the exception of food, nearly every item can go through two or more cycles of use. The **first cycle** is for its intended purpose: a can holds oil, a cardboard carton holds rolls of toilet paper, a plastic bottle holds bleach, a tire upholds a car. In the **next cycle** a can is beaten into a toy or candle holder, a cardboard box is unfolded to make a child's sleeping pallet, a bleach bottle now holds drinking water, and the tire may go to make sandals, an art project or a fiery street blockade! The item will go through continued cycles until cartons dissolve in muddy paste, bottles spring leaks, and wire and fiber poke out of the tires. When the item has absolutely no further use, it is thrown into the street.

Paper, rusty cans, ragged tires, shredded plastic bags, broken bottles, and containers litter the streets and chickens, goats, pigs, and dogs root through the jumble looking for a morsel of food. Some roads are downright impassable because trash and junk block the street.

Since the recycling company opened, *brouettes* and some small trucks, loaded beyond capacity with metal or plastic, lumber down the streets of Port-au-Prince. Curious about how the recycling process in Haiti is done, I followed several men who had *brouettes*. Since junk is everywhere, the collection stage is fairly easy. With a full load they pull the *brouette* through traffic to wait in a long line at the recycling site. Each cart is pulled onto a scale to determine the loaded weight. After being weighed, the cart has a number painted on it and the worker proceeds to a dumping point. Dumping sounds easy, but it takes a lot of pulling to release the load from the cart. Assorted wire and metal strips bind the refuse together and make it hard to move off the cart.

Finally, with the cargo unloaded, the weary, sweat-drenched man must pull the cart to yet another line and wait to have the empty cart weighed. Then, with a payment voucher in hand, he waits again to receive money. I calculated several payments and not one came to more than $20US. After hours and hours of back-breaking, energy draining work the man pulls the cart back home with $20 or less in his pocket. If he had helpers, he must pay these men from his earnings. If he has time before sunset, he will begin gathering and loading the cart for the next day.

Haiti snow days

In northern climates snow days shut down schools and businesses, halt transportation and keep people inside their homes. You might ask, "How can you have a snow day in Haiti?" In Haiti we have two classes of "snow days." Light snow days close schools

73

and some small businesses. Heavy snow days close everything: schools, businesses, government offices, markets, and even the roadside vendors.

The snow in Haiti doesn't fall in pure white crystals but flakes of soot and ash. This snow does not originate from weather patterns but from discontentment and political unrest. Demonstrations and manifestations marked by fiery blockades fill the air with smoke and the stench of burning tires.

You'll never have to deal with treacherous ice in Haiti, but venturing out on a Haitian snow day may mean having your car flipped over by a mob and the windows smashed. Reminders of Haiti's snow days don't fade with time. Skeletons of burned out cars and seared and scorched pavements mark the location of the scores of uprisings. Those "snow-day" piles do not melt after the storm but are constant reminders of how quickly a blizzard of destruction can endanger your life.

Many snow days come without warning, so I had to engage a weather team. I call one member of the team Daniel Boone. Boone was a wilderness pioneer who knew the signs of American Indians. My Daniel Boone accompanies me and keeps alert for smoke signals that mark demonstrations and danger. With his help, I take back roads and side streets to get to my destination – often the US Consulate. My weather team also helps me determine if blocked traffic is due to an accident or a demonstration.

Even more dangerous are empty streets. On days that the streets are empty, street markets vacant, and businesses closed with security bars still in place, we know the people are hunkering down waiting for an explosion of violence. It is like a warning running across the bottom of the TV screen – Storm Warning. Riot Conditions.

Even though I and my "weather team" stayed alert we still got caught on some heavy snow days. My car, Betsy, bears the scars of these encounters. Her windows have been smashed out with rocks so many times that I just decided to replace the windows with metal grates. She looks like a store front in a heavy crime area in New York City. She doesn't provide much protection in gunfire, but she does keep the rocks out.

The day Port-au-Prince stood still

Haitian culture is full of fears that discourage and control the people. Fear feeds anarchy and anger and kills the spirit of the people. On February 26, 1998, I witnessed the power of fear as it touched almost every person in Haiti. This fear caused millions in economic loss due to closed businesses and loss of personal income and this fear even caused the death of several people. To make matters worse, government and influential people in Haiti deliberately promoted the people's fear. What could be so frightening that it affected the lives and welfare of a country?

An eclipse.

Business stopped. Stores closed. Markets emptied. Nothing moved on the streets. A friend made the usual two-hour trip to Carrefour in 13 minutes. One radio broadcast predicted that even the rats feared coming out of their holes. Warnings were issued, "If you go out, you will go blind. If you leave your home you'll get AIDS. If rain falls on you, you may get leprosy." Terrified, the people locked themselves indoors and covered their windows. Families, fearfully huddled inside. Closed off from fresh air, many suffocated in the tropical noon-day heat.

Is fear a powerful weapon? Yes it is!

MAKE THAT BABY HAPPY!

CHAPTER 11

Building Blocks

During my time in Haiti, I placed more than 1500 children in adoptive homes. Although each one was blessed with a unique personality, many of their stories were similar. One or both parents had died or the living parents could not afford to feed the child. Infants were abandoned at Ruuska gate, at orphanages, or on the streets. Almost all suffered from malnutrition and would have surely died before their first birthday.

Discarded on the trash heap

Saraha was thrown onto a pile of garbage on the street when she was an infant. A lady found her and cared for her until she was eight years old. Saraha completed two years of school before she was sold as a household worker to an unkind and difficult woman. Her schooling ended and she spent the next four years washing clothes, cooking, and cleaning.

At age 12 a woman named Carole assisted Saraha in finding her birth family. Her unmarried parents were no longer together but both had many more children and there was no place for Saraha.

She found shelter with a cousin but soon became pregnant by an eighteen-year-old young man who could provide no support.

When Sawens was born, Saraha knew nothing about raising a baby. After all, she was a child herself. She had no financial help and could not even purchase milk for the infant when her milk ran dry. Saraha kept Sawens as long as she could but eventually a friend brought her and the baby to Ruuska Village for adoption. Sawens was chosen for adoption very quickly by a couple in Argentina that also adopted another boy at the same time.

I invited Saraha to live at Ruuska Village. Despite being a little shy Saraha got along with the other women. She began working as a nanny for two older children and when they go to their new adopted home, she will start school. Ruuska Village gave Saraha a home and hope. She has a plan for her future, and is taking sewing, pedicure and craft classes that we provide. She even makes a little money by selling bracelets that she makes. Saraha loves God and attends church. She said, "I prayed for a good home for Sawens and myself, and God answered my prayers." She says that she will not have any more babies until God finds her a good husband.

Almost twins

Dieuna's father died when she was eight and her mother died when she was 12. She was the oldest of seven children and lived with her aunt for five years. Dieuna's first child was Woodley Dorvilus and his father helped with most of the child's needs. Since Dieuna had family in the United States the child went to live with them in Miami, Florida.

Dieuna then began working for a family in Lissen. She helped cook, clean and care for three children, but when she was seventeen she became pregnant with her second child. The father's family cared for little Ralph, but Dieuna kept moving from one job to another and from one man to another. When a third child was born to Dieuna, the woman for whom she was working offered to raise baby Richardson as her own. Richardson was well cared for and went to school.

Eventually Dieuna moved into a new home with a new man and gave birth to Calens, her fourth child. Finally, Dieuna's life had stabilized. Calens' father had work and she cared for the little boy. On January 12, 2010, though, the earthquake struck killing Dieuna's husband and destroying their home.

As thousands of other homeless Haitians, Dieuna lived in a tent. She had no work, no food, or even clean water for three-month-old Calens. A woman living in a nearby tent told Dieuna about Ruuska Village.

When Dieuna came to the village and told us her story, we accepted Calens for adoption and quickly found a home for Calens in Argentina. Dieuna, then, found work with a woman who treated her kindly, but Dieuna fled the home and work when the husband tried to rape her. She returned to Daniel Gabriel, the father of her second child and of course was soon pregnant again. She returned to Ruuska Village with the baby that she had given the same name as her third child, Richardson.

The second Richardson had been born with bi-lateral club feet. The family that chose him consulted doctors and a hospital and agreed to provide the necessary care to straighten his legs. This couple had no children and decided to adopt Donald Maki at the same time.

I knew that Dieuna would never escape the cycle of searching for love and then getting pregnant unless she had the stability of a home, so I invited her to live and work at Ruuska. There she worked as a nanny, began schooling, and studied craft art, sewing, and how to do pedicures.

Not even a note

Unlike Richardson, Donald Maki had not been brought to us by a parent with the hope of the child having a better life. Donald Maki was found in a pile of garbage on the street of Delmas. There was no note or information left with him leaving us with no way of learning more about this baby boy with bright brown eyes, curly hair and a toothless smile.

Once discovered, he had been taken to IBESR (Social Services of Haiti). They called Crèche du Ciel Bleu requesting that we take him into our orphanage and we agreed. We received the baby accompanied by documents from the Conseil Municipal de la Croix des Bouquets stating he was found on the street abandoned and left to die.

We named the month-old baby Donald Maki and were able to acquire a placement certificate from IBESR. Changes in adoption policies following the quake, however, seriously slowed the adoption process. In time the paper work was finished and both Donald and Richardson went to their new home. The boys were almost like twins because of their ages, but were quite different in temperament. Donald was quiet, calm and loved to be cuddled, while Richardson was very active and constantly in motion.

We know God has a plan for these boys and they will flourish with their new family. Their testimonies will truly show God's great grace and speak volumes to everyone who hears their stories. We were blessed to be a part of their life stories.

When two agree

In 1996 I was living in Carrefour helping to care for a guest home. One day, two ladies came to me and asked if I could adopt out a very pretty little girl named Venette. They had her birth certificate and explained that they had no room in their orphanage for her. This sweet little girl's mother and father were both dead. Her mother had died giving birth to her ninth baby just a month ago. Unfortunately, that baby had passed away as well. With eight children and no parents, one more child was too much for the extended family to handle.

I made arrangements to meet the two ladies in Gonaïves, where the family lived. They took me to a house with many children and I met several children from that family. Two of the siblings were five and seven and Venette was three. Many children in Haiti have never seen a white person and are often a bit afraid of them. Venette, unlike many, was not afraid of me. When I called her over she sat on my lap without a problem. She had a sad look on her face, but welcomed my friendly face. I thought, "This could work. She likes me!"

After we sat for a bit, I decided to take her outside and have her sit on the motorcycle that I had traveled on to Gonaïves. I put her hands on the bars and made fake motor sounds. It didn't scare her at all, so I had the driver turn it on. She showed no fear.

With Venette tucked in between the driver and me, we made the three-hour trip to Carrefour with Venette. We made occasional stops for beverages along the way but didn't get home until dark. Venette took the adventure with no fuss and I think she actually enjoyed it. A family in Kansas wanted to adopt a child, so Venette already had a home and family ready to take her.

The next day, I took Venette with me when I went to the airport to meet the mission aviation service that brought in supplies and mail. Joe Hurston was also waiting for the plane. Joe Hurston describes that encounter in his book *Run to the Roar: Stories About Facing Tough Challenges Head-On.*

> One day while I was waiting at the Port-au-Prince airport for Dr. Helmer's DC3 to arrive with supplies and a fifteen-member mission team, Barbara Walker joined me. Barbara, a frequent

guest in our home, had never accepted the idea that women are the "weaker sex." If something needed to be done—like moving a wandering bull off the road—she would take the bull by the horns and move it. The word *helpless* was not in her personal vocabulary even after major surgeries. Her ministry, however, focused on the truly helpless—orphan children in Haiti. She tracked down helpless and hopeless children and arranged for their adoption by American couples.

Today, as usual, she had a child in tow. While we waited for the plane, I watched the adorable three-year-old girl energetically climb on the railing outside the door to customs. When I caught her eye, she smiled shyly. Barbara had brought many orphans through our home, but this one seemed special. I felt a special tug at my heart when she smiled at me.

"What's the story on her?" I asked Barbara.

"She's from Sous Chaud (translated "hot water") on the northwestern coast."

"I've been there," I said. "Barren mountain ranges, cracked earth, mud huts. They have to walk an hour and a half or two to get water."

"More like three hours," Barbara said.

"What happened?"

"Her mother died while giving birth to her ninth child. The baby died, too….She's the youngest child, and there is no one to care for her."

Thank God, Barbara found her. I didn't know how she did it, but she found these little ones and rescued them. We talked, and I watched the little girl bounce around. Then I asked, "Barbara, is she spoken for?"

"Yes, I already have a family for her."

"Have they seen her? Have they had any contact with her yet?"

"Not yet."

"Find another little girl for those people."

Barbara turned and looked at me with raised eyebrows.

I just smiled.

The plane landed, and we loaded trucks with supplies and team members and headed for Gressier. Barbara, as she often did, accompanied the team and me. No matter how well organized, chaos reigns during the first hours of a team's arrival. Unloading supplies, giving instructions on water, toilets, showers, and sleeping accommodations, and answering the same questions fifteen times generate noise and confusion.

While I put supplies away and focused on directing team members to their accommodations on the porch, in tents, or under the stars, Cindy and Barbara, with the little girl at their heels, prepared food for the travelers. In the kitchen, I saw Cindy nod toward the little girl and ask Barbara questions. Cindy appeared to show a special interest in the child.

I knew that with a team in our home, days would pass before Cindy and I could have a normal, relaxed, uninterrupted conversation, so I stopped storing supplies and said, "Cindy, could I speak with you a minute?" I nodded toward our bedroom. In our room I asked, "What do you think of this little girl?" Cindy looked at me like—well, we knew at that very moment we felt the same about her. "What do you think?" I said.

"I think we need to adopt her," Cindy said.

"So do I."

From that moment on, we considered ourselves the parents of this little girl that we named Juliet Joy. Barbara agreed to find another child for the adopting couple, and we began the process of jumping through legal hoops to adopt Juliet.

Cindy, like Joe, had also instantly fallen in love with the little girl. After talking about the adoption, they insisted she stay with them in their home while I began to process the paperwork. They also asked what would become of her five-year-old sister, Dieulila. I reassured them that she too would find a loving home.

Joe soon called his sister, Mary, in Michigan and told her that they would be adopting Venette. They told her about Venette's sister, Dieulila, and suggested she adopt Dieulila so both of the sisters could be in the USA. Joe's sister agreed and so the adoption process began.

Perdition

One of the first things to do was the lab tests to see if both of the girls had any problems. All of the tests came back normal. I made arrangements to meet with the god mother for the required abandonment papers and death certificates. She said it would not be a problem for the mother's death certificate because it was only three months ago, but the father's would be difficult because he had died eight years ago. The god mother told me someone in the family might have it.

I found it odd that the mother had given birth to four of her husband's children after he died. I told my translator "I don't believe this story. How can she have four children by her "husband" when he's been dead eight years?"

"Oh, no Barbara," he explained, "this happens in Haiti. When the father dies, the shock and grief are so hard on the pregnant mother that she goes into **perdition**."

"She what!"

"Yes, often the pregnancy will be put on hold for up to three years before the baby is born."

Well, the mother must have been pregnant with quadruplets because she had a seven-year- old boy, five and three-year-old girls, and she had died giving birth to her last child. Yes, indeed, everyone in Haiti knows about this "perdition!" Well, no matter what, we needed a death certificate for the "father." The father's brother had signed for the death certificate, meaning he could sign for permission of the adoption.

Next stop was the physical requirements. I took Venette to Dr. Pape, a great German doctor that was approved by the American Consulate to do visa physicals. I put her up on the table and gave him her birth certificate and lab test results. Dr. Pape was a talker. He always had time to talk about the child and it didn't take long for him to ask the story behind Venette. I told him about her parents and that she had recently been put into my care. As soon as I told him about the death of her parents, he said, "Oh! Perdition!"

I could not believe my ears!

"Don't even try to tell the people **perdition** did not happen," he said. "Perdition is quite common in Haiti. I regularly see women who say they have been pregnant for two or three years."

Well, Venette (Juliet Joy) and Dieulila finished up their adoption without any more bumps in the road and soon went to live in the USA. They have grown into lovely and talented young women and have truly made their adoptive families proud.

CHAPTER 12

Doors to Hope

Restaveks

The practice of poor families giving away children to wealthier acquaintances or relatives is known in the native Creole as "restavek," from the French words rester avec, or "to stay with." Critics call it slavery. The children, they said, are taken in as servants, forced to work without pay, isolated from other children in the household and seldom sent to school. (Reuters)

"A restavek is a child placed in domestic slavery," said Jean-Robert Cadet, a former restavek who now runs a foundation to improve the lives of restavek children. (www.restavekfreedom.org).

Gerlande Gerlin Bellegarde's father had passed away. Her mother, with thirteen children, lived in a ten by ten mud-plastered shack up in the mountains. They never had enough food. The children did not attend school, and had only rags for clothing.

The mother gave up two of her children, including Gerlande, to work as household servants. Gerlande cleaned, cooked, carried water, washed clothes, and tried her best to please the family she served. Although she tried her best, her best was never good enough for this family. She was beaten for not working hard enough and after months of abuse ran away. She went to the police station and told them her story and they handed her over to IBESR to be placed in an orphanage.

IBESR called us and asked if we could care for six-year-old Gerlande. We accepted her, sight unseen. Gerlande was pretty and polite, but a bit frightened, which was normal for a child who had endured such horrible experiences. She seemed to be closer to eight years old, however, than six.

Gerlande told our social worker that she loved her birth family, but did not want to go back to them. She agreed to stay in our village until someone would adopt her. She loved going to school and brought joy to everyone with her bright, sweet smile. In preparation for adoption we did the necessary doctor visits, lab tests, social worker interviews, and a psychologist examination, which all came back acceptable. Before allowing her to be adopted we went in search for Gerlande's biological family. She seemed to have a good idea where they lived, so Mirlande and Lucien took her to find her family's home. It was a six-hour journey on a mountainous route along the Dominican border. After driving down river beds and crossing knee-high water they finally arrived at Gerlande's home.

Gerlande was happy to see her mother and family, but they were shocked to see her. The family Gerlande served had told them that Gerlande had been kidnapped and her heart had been stolen. They had grieved for her loss and were now overjoyed that she was safe. Gerlande explained to her family and the neighborhood friends that had gathered that she had been abused and ran away. Shortly after she told her story, the man who had beaten her showed up. Had it not been for the intervention of a pastor, the crowd would have killed the man.

Gerlande told her mother and siblings that she wanted to stay in our village and be adopted into the USA. She explained to them that she had good food, went to school, had nice clothing, toys, and **her very own bed.**

After the family reunion we invited Gerlande's mother to visit us at the village. The mother showed up at the gates of our village two weeks later with some of her family and she began "signing" the required paperwork so Gerlande could be adopted. During this process, we asked about Gerlande's age. Unfortunately, her mother did not know. She explained that she had given birth to so many children that she did not know all the ages. We could only assign a birthdate to Gerlande and have a birth certificate made for her. The date of her birth had not been significant to her birth family, but Gerlande would go to a family that would celebrate her birthday.

With the print of her thumb, Gerlande's mother gives permission for Gerlande's future adoption.
Photography by <u>audreydewys.com</u>

Political dilemma

Meranna Ambroise, like so many pregnant moms, came to me for help. I gave her vitamins and did lab tests. She came back many times telling me she wanted to give me her baby. I told her that I wasn't taking any babies but that she could return if she needed help with doctors and medicine.

While I was in the US for back surgery, she had her baby. When I returned to Haiti, she spotted me in Port-au-Prince during the first week that I was back.

"Here is your baby," she said, extending a bundle wrapped in a terry cloth towel.

"No, he is not my baby. He is **your** baby."

After a few rounds of this conversation, she said, "You **must** take this baby!"

"No, **you must** care for him."

She replied, "No, he is an **American baby**, he is **your** baby."

"What do you mean, 'He is an **American** baby?' He's a Haitian baby."

"I named him John Kerry, so he is an American baby."

What a dilemma!

Should we look for a Democrat to adopt him? Or can we find a sympathetic Republican that would adopt him in spite of his name?

Bumblebee

On February 20, 2003, Modeline Louis gave birth to premature twins. One baby died shortly after birth. The surviving twin, named Sedeline was a low-weight baby. The infant battled difficulties right away. Due to esophageal reflux most of what she ate came back up through her nose. Each feeding put her at risk of aspirating and dying. Since she retained very little nourishment she didn't grow. When she was two months old, she was brought to us for care. She weighed four pounds. I placed her in my best foster home, the one we nicknamed "the fat farm." She still did not do well.

At that time, Kindra and Hannah came to Haiti to help me. They agreed to care for Sedeline who was soon nicknamed "Bumblebee." They fed her small amounts often, and in an upright position, and carefully burped and walked her most of the day and night. I filled in each day by rocking and singing her to sleep. Care for Sedeline required three caregivers but she finally began to grow. Other than being a dermatologist's nightmare, she was basically healthy.

An American family immediately chose Sedeline for adoption and the mother came to Haiti to help care for her. The woman, though had to be emergency evacuated from Haiti due to pain and hemorrhaging of a tubular pregnancy. Hannah also had to return to the states and Bumblebee kept Kindra and me working long hours. It was a long haul but Sept. 23, 2003, Sedeline got her visa and went to her new family in the USA. Although, she still had problems with food, she developed into a beautiful and healthy child.

A weeping father

Wilmarck Georges, of half-Cuban descent, and Guerda Dubois lived in Ouanaminthe, a town bordering the Dominican Republic. They requested to be married and presented their birth certificates to the church and were waiting until they would be allowed to marry. During the waiting period Esther was born. When Esther was fifteen days old, her mother boarded a boat with hopes of escaping Haiti and finding a better life in the US. The boat sank. Everyone perished.

Wilmarck cared for Esther the best he could. He borrowed money for formula and diapers. He got into trouble with many people because of his desperate need for milk and supplies for Esther. He couldn't work and care for the child so he went to the local children's home to ask for help. They helped as much as they could but suggested allowing her to be adopted by an American family.

On November 10, 2003, Wilmarck brought three-month old Esther to me. She was a chubby, beautiful, good-natured little girl. Papa Wilmarck wept as he told me his story. He told Kindra and me how very much he loved Esther's mom and how difficult it was to let go of Esther. He went with us for the lab tests, doctor exams, psychological testing. When it came time to sign the abandonment papers, he repeatedly broke down in tears. The judge assured Wilnick that it was best for the baby and the only way of providing the care she needed to survive.

This process was emotional for Kindra and me also. We usually dealt with people who smiled and acted relieved to give away their child. Kindra and I wanted to say, "Keep her and we will support you," but we couldn't. I couldn't guarantee I would be in Haiti or be able to provide for her until she was an adult. Adoption was the only real answer.

Baking soda not recommended for EVERYTHING

On November 5, 2000, I was at my office in Port-au-Prince, Haiti. It had been a very hot, very busy day and I was exhausted. Just as I decided to go home a little early, Pastor Joelle walked in to tell me the story of a mother and child that were in crisis. He explained that the mother had come to my office several times but had not been able to find me. She was a single mother with a one-year old son named Wilky. On September 22, she had given birth to a little girl, Farah. They lived with the grandmother, but there was very little income to feed this family and the new baby was extremely thin. If we didn't get the baby today, she would probably die. Having no other choice, we went with Pastor Joelle to Marianni, a small town just west of Port-au-Prince.

When we arrived, I met the mother — a very tall, thin, pretty lady. She was excited to see us and brought us directly to the room where the baby was sleeping. There was a cloth on the floor where Wilky and Farah both lay sound asleep. The mother picked up little Farah and put her in my hands. "You can have her," she said.

Farah was 26 inches long and weighed 4 ½ pounds with her clothes on.

"When was she born?" I asked.

"September 22nd," she said. Pointing to the little boy, she said, "Wilky was one year old on the 13th."

"What have you been feeding the baby?"

"I had two babies in one year and I couldn't feed them both, " she said. "I put baking soda in water for her."

How could this child have survived so long on baking soda? Pastor Joelle surely had not exaggerated the needs of this child. Farah was so thin and weak I told the mother, "I'll take her but she may not survive." Farah was so malnourished and dehydrated I nearly cried at the sight of her.

We left with Farah and stopped at the pharmacy to get Pedialyte, a bottle, and a 2cc syringe to feed her with if she refused to suck on the bottle. Sometimes when a child is seriously malnourished they are too weak to suck on the bottle or they have simply given up and refuse to eat. This was definitely not the case with Farah. She sucked the entire bottle up like a Hoover vacuum.

I took her back to my home and Rita cared for her all night. We also started her on four ounces of formula that night. We had to be careful not to shock her system with the introduction of real food. Farah, though, never had a problem. She eagerly ate everything that was offered. Early the next morning I asked if she felt better with something in her tummy. She looked directly at me and smiled from ear to ear showing deep dimples. Farah seemed advanced for her age.

We took Farah to the doctor for a checkup and Dr. Carre expressed concern.

"Don't bother with the lab tests," she said. "This baby won't be alive by the time you get the results back."

"Do the tests." I said. "God did not send her to me for nothing. He has a plan for her and I will do my best to keep her alive." A few days later we began to see tremendous improvement. "Farah is going to make it," I said.

Rita and her family are our best caregivers and Rita was willing to accept this challenge, so we packed up tiny Farah and her supplies and went to Cap-Haitian. I invited Farah's mom to come and also bring Wilky for HIV testing.

"I want to keep Wilky," the mother said.

"That's fine," I told her, "but let's get him tested anyway."

I gave her clothing, milk, and vitamins for Wilky and told her to come back in a week for the test results. When the lab results came in, Mom was HIV positive, but Wilky was negative. I told the mother "Wilky is OK but he should not drink your milk anymore. I will give you formula. Come back when you need more and be sure to let me know if he becomes sick. We will make sure he gets medical care."

Farah's test results were not as encouraging. This poor little thing, living for 45 days on baking soda and water, nearly starved to death, and now we find that she too is HIV positive. Most people don't know much about HIV and AIDS and the difference between the two, and are instantly afraid to even touch a child that is HIV positive. Rita and her family, however, cared for tiny Farah and she began to grow.

Farah was never sick and proved to be far more advanced than normal for a baby her age, even a healthy, well fed baby. She sat up early, got her baby seat rocking so fast that we were afraid she was going to flip right out of it. We started her in a Jolly Jumper early and were all amazed at just how high those things can actually bounce. It was amazing the transformation from a tiny, thin, half-dead baby into a happy, healthy, strong, and quite smart child with dimples big enough to hide quarters in. Later, I joked about it saying "I have discovered the secret to smart kids. Start them out on nothing but baking soda."

Although Farah was growing and energetic, we were still concerned about her positive HIV testing. A child is born with the mother's antibodies. If the mother is HIV positive, the child will test HIV positive for up to 18 months before these antibodies are expelled and the child then "converts" to HIV negative. We took Farah for HIV testing several times, truly believing that our prayers would be answered and she would convert to negative. Farah was tested on April 4th and showed trace amounts of HIV. The doctor said that the next time should be it and on June 28th— Praise the Lord— Farah was retested and came out HIV negative.

Many people had been praying for Farah. She will never know how many prayers were offered to God on her behalf, but she will surely know how much God loves her. Farah is absolutely a very special child chosen by God's hand and elected into the family of His love. I have no doubt that He has an equally special plan in mind for her life.

The rest of Farah's story.

Kindra came to visit me in Haiti. While here, she helped care for Christelle and Gabriel, two children who were living at my home. Each child had a nickname. We called Christelle "Thumbelina" because she was a perfect miniature child. At six months she weighed seven pounds and was only twenty inches long. Gabriel, two weeks younger than Christelle, was known as the Jolly Green Giant because he was huge.

Kindra's parents had been talking about adopting, but hadn't actually started the process. Kindra quickly fell in love with Christelle and Gabriel, but Gabriel was already assigned to a family and would be traveling to the US very soon. Christelle, however, was not growing. She seemed happy, but we were very concerned. I took her to several different doctors only to find that she was normal for her age in everything but size and strength. Kindra was also very interested in little Farah. She hadn't met her yet, but she had heard the miraculous stories.

Kindra called her parents and told them about Christelle and they soon called back to say that they had prayed about it and had decided to adopt Christelle. During our conversation I suggested that they might consider two children. I was thinking that they might want an older child to fill in the gap between their youngest who was 10 and Christelle who was not yet a year old.

"We have discussed adopting two children," they said, "but if we adopt another we would like to adopt Farah. She had a bad start but she is a fighter."

Unexpected Delays

By early September 2001, Christelle and Farah's adoptions were finished and the new family came to Haiti to take their babies home. After all the things that Farah had to overcome, it looked like she was finally on her way to the US to start her new life. Then came September 11th and as our own country stood in shock, all they could do was wait, stuck in Haiti, unable to leave because airplanes were grounded.

I have encountered unbelievable days in Haiti while attempting to get children into the hands of their new parents, but this time the parents had the children, they just couldn't get them home. While they waited, the family dealt with fear, stress, disappointment, and even personal tragedy as they were notified that the grandmother had died. They also missed the wedding shower of the oldest daughter as they waited to return. Furthermore, the INS was closed. Even if they could get a flight out, no visas were being signed. It seemed worse every day. Everyone was ready to break down and cry.

How did we get through those terrible days? Only by the peace and grace of God. Our faith calmed our fears and God's gift of grace soothed our weary spirits, giving us the patience we so desperately needed. And, through this distressing time, Farah continued to bring joy too all of us. She continued to grow and started taking a few steps here and there. Four days later she was nearly running. She amazed and amused all of us as we waited. Finally the airlines reopened, INS started signing visas, and Farah, Christelle, and their new family left just in time to attend their new sister's wedding. And as the saying goes, "they lived happily ever after."

Mama Chicklet

Jeannette Cadet, a mother of four children, has been coming to our village for several years. We call her "Mamma Chicklet."

Because of the hard times in Haiti, Jeannette came to the Ruuska Village asking us to adopt her daughter, Magdalie, who was born August 21, 2004. We checked into her family's living conditions and found that they were all hungry and in need of medical assistance. We accepted her daughter, Magdalie, for adoption and proceeded with the process. During the adoption process Magdalie stayed at the village and Jeannette came every two weeks for a bag of *Feed the Starving Children* meal packs, which were supplied to us from *Love A Child* ministries here in Haiti.

When Jeannette came for her food, she always brought a gift of three packages of Chicklets, so before long we nicknamed Jeannette's daughter, Magdalie, "Chicklet" and we called Jeannette "Mamma Chicklet."

Magdalie (Chicklet) now lives in Argentina with her adoptive family; they also adopted a Haitian boy named Calens and another Haitian girl named Melissa. Magdalie has two Haitian families;

the mother and siblings she left behind in Haiti and her new Haitian siblings in Argentina.

Mamma Chicklet still comes every two weeks for some food and still brings her special gift of three packs of Chicklets. Along with weekly food, Mamma Chicklet receives photos and news about Chicklet's new life. We also help her other children by providing school bags full of supplies once a year. Along with shoes and clothing we assist them with medical care. Mamma Chicklet is friendly, grateful, and always has a smile.

Maki—Maki—Maki —EVERYWHERE

Many people question why so many children have the name of Maki. My maiden name was Maki. My father never had any boys to carry on the name, so I took it on myself to carry on the name.

Many children come to us without birth certificates and legal names. At first we had Maki as a given name for boys and then we used it as a middle name. Later, it seemed that Maki Lu and Maki Lynn sounded pretty good too so we used it for some girls.

As I got older my personality went from strange to unique and now eccentric, I felt the need to graft the Maki family tree into a Haitian family tree. My father had two brothers; Edward Maki and Eric Maki. So, I gave each name to a baby. Uncle Eric has three children: Brian, Jerilyn and Geraldlyn. I have already used the names of Brian Maki and Jerilyn Maki for babies and maybe someday I will have a Geraldlyn Maki too.

My Uncle Edward had ten children. I have used several of his children's names for my babies: Donald Maki, James Maki, Bruce Maki and Victor Maki.

My favorites of course are Lauri Maki and Alicia Maki named after my parents. These children are both in Argentina with more than ten children sharing the family name.

Many times mothers bring babies to me for adoption. They tell me that I must accept the child because the baby's name is Maki. Some adoptive parents have even changed their child's name to Maki after the adoption as a pleasant gesture to me. One thing for sure, the Maki name will endure for a while.

Cabbage Patch Kid

James Maki came to our village on November 21, 2013. The first time I laid eyes on him I instantly realized he looked like the famous Cabbage Patch doll. He had short curly hair, two tiny round eyes, and high puffy cheeks. Everything about him was a spitting image of a Cabbage Patch Kid. Even his mouth was identical!

Charite Elusme, James' mother, was thirty-one years old and not married. She also had two other children: Dave, who was twelve, Michela, who was nine, and now James, who was not yet a month old. The mother was unable to produce milk for James, which made it difficult to provide for him because milk is so expensive in Haiti. Charite explained that she had a job selling goods on the street, but had no one to look after her baby boy. She was already fighting to provide food, schooling, and clothing for her two older kids and knew she could not provide for her new baby.

We began the appropriate lab tests, doctor appointments, psychology interviews, and social worker interviews. The results came back showing both the mother and baby were healthy. We were excited about having this sweet boy in our village. This excitement actually reminded me of my own daughters' joy when opening up their very own Cabbage Patch dolls on Christmas morning.

We had so much fun with this little boy. He was one of the first babies I showed off when new visitors arrived. Everyone who saw this baby boy were in total agreement— he was identical to a Cabbage Patch doll!

"Cabbage Patch," as we called him, was adopted by a family in Indiana who had already adopted two Haitian girls from me. This family will surely provide a good life for him and teach him to love himself, love his family, and most important to love God. What more could we want for our sweet Cabbage Patch doll?

James "Cabbage Patch" Maki.
Photography by <u>audreydewys.com</u>

CHAPTER 13

Beauty Out of Ashes

Some little girls have survived against such impossible odds that I wanted to give them special recognition and began crowning a Reach Out to Haiti Princess each year. Dressed in frills and bows and crowned with a tiny tiara, the little ones became poster children for Reach Out to Haiti. One little girl served a unique purpose of ministering to a grieving couple.

In all things, God is at work

Ilonese brought her granddaughter to me when Jennifer was only a few weeks old. Grandma explained that Jennifer's mother was "a crazy street lady" and couldn't care for a baby. Tragically, this had not always been the case. Jennifer's mother had been an intelligent, educated and attractive woman until she was injured in a car accident. The doctors had done the best that they could, but the mother had suffered a head trauma that left her confused and unpredictable. The grandmother explained that Jennifer's mother would leave for long periods of time, then come back as if nothing had happened. After Jennifer's father died, her mother started living on the streets.

A friend had found Jennifer's mother with a new baby and taken her back to Bon Repos to the house she had lived in before her husband died. To the dismay of the friend, Jennifer's mother put a corn cob in the infant's mouth and lay her in a mud puddle in front of the house and walked away. The friend picked up the baby, washed off the mud and took her to Grandmother Ilonese.

Ilonese, however, was already caring for two young children and had to sell tea in the market each day to put food on the table. She could not work and care for an infant at the same time. Someone told her about Ruuska Village, so she brought Jennifer and asked if we could find someone to adopt her.

I'm not a real emotional person, but I almost cried when I saw Jennifer. She was a beautiful, light complexioned child but had burn marks on one arm and leg. Ilonese explained, "I made a little fire to keep the mosquitoes away from the children. One of the children knocked the fire over and it fell on Jennifer."

Obviously, caring for a baby that young, along with her other responsibilities was more than Ilonese could handle. Of course we took Jennifer in and started doctor and lab tests. In spite of her tough start to life, she was healthy and her burns healed quickly.

A family immediately asked to adopt Jennifer, so we started searching for her mother to get consent to the adoption. We searched and searched for the mother, but couldn't find her. After months of jumping through legal hoops, Jennifer was finally approved for adoption and left for her new home in the States.

The family that adopted her was anxious to get her home. During the adoption process they had discovered their young son had a brain tumor that would soon take his life. One of the boy's last wishes was that he could see his new sister. She arrived in time to spend time with him before the tumor took his life and he went to be with God.

No one can imagine the suffering that this entire family went through during this time, but God knew their path and had led them to adopt before they were even aware that they would lose their son. I know that Jennifer was never meant to replace their son, but she was a gift from God, sent to comfort them during their time of grief.

This family will have many wonderful memories of their son, and I know in my heart that one of their most cherished will be of the smile on his face when he got his wish and saw his sister for the first time.

I think maybe this year the princess title fell a bit short of the mark; perhaps "angel" would be a bit more accurate. In any event, mere words fail to define the blessings in God's great plan for us all. God is always at work bringing good out of all things that we face. Out of the tragedy of a mother's brain injury, God brought comfort to a family that lost a son to a brain tumor.

You Can't Stop Me

When Renette gave birth to twins the father considered Renette selfish. According to his philosophy, no one should have two babies at one time, so he killed one. When Renette again gave birth to twins he again killed one. When Renette again got pregnant and had Mickerline she feared for the baby's life.

Renette brought her to me saying, "All I want is for my baby to have a good life and be loved."

I gladly accepted the tiny two-month old baby, but Mickerline soon became sick with a fever, anemia and pneumonia and had to be hospitalized. With shaved head, IVs in her head, hands and feet, I wondered if she would make it, but when she opened her eyes, I knew instantly that she was a survivor. Her brown eyes sparkled and brimmed with spirit and strength. They fairly shouted, "I'm going to make it and you can't stop me!"

We expected to take her home soon. Instead of releasing her, though, the hospital told us that they were going to do a blood transfusion. We had no control over her care and felt helpless, scared and frustrated. Her chances of surviving a seemingly unnecessary blood transfusion were slim to zero. All we could do was pray. And pray, we did.

Several days later we received the call to, "Come and get her."

"What?" I asked.

"We cancelled the transfusion, she can go home."

It was one of those moments when I felt that overwhelming desire to jump up and down, laugh, and cry all at once. Hallelujah!! Does the Lord answer prayer? Yes!!! Times like these remind us of how powerful our God is. Once again we thanked God for intervening and giving another little one a chance at life. We picked up Mickerline from the hospital and brought her back to Bon Repo where we began caring for her.

Mickerline was a spitfire with a zest for life even at a young age. She radiated life and joy. She was the sweetest, happiest baby ever and had a smile to match. She quickly filled out and within a month had reached 10 pounds. Renette came often to inquire about her baby. She could barely contain her excitement when she saw how Mickerline was blooming.

Mickerline was without a doubt in our minds, a special angel chosen by God to live life. And so we crowned her Reach Out to Haiti Princess of 2002.

A couple in Minnesota adopted Mickerline and also adopted three more Haitian children. She grew up in a loving Christian home and had Haitian siblings. God had granted Renette the desire of her heart. Her little girl had a good life and lots of love. Story endings like this made our work rewarding and encourage us to continue trying to give others a better chance in life.

Miss America 2011 crowns a princess

Following the earthquake in 2010, Miss America 2011, Teresa Scalan, visited Haiti and honored us by crowning our Reach Out to Haiti Princess of 2011. Miss America actually placed her crown on Jenica Elysee's head and officially named her Princess Jenica.

Jenica Elysee was born May 25, 2011, and came to Ruuska Village on June 18, 2011. She came with her mother, father, and two sisters, Islande, age five and Christella, age twelve. She also had a brother, Libernode, age seven. The father had an electoral card stating he was 48 years old, and the mother had a birth certificate and ID card showing her age as 41. The parents had come to ask if someone could adopt some of the children.

"Our life is difficult," the father explained. "The children are often hungry. We can only afford to send one child to school."

Baby Jenica and her sisters and brother were lovely children, but I could not take them all in. I told the parents, "I do not bring older children into Ruuska Village as I do not normally have adoption opportunities for twelve-year-old girls, and I do not take in boys over one year.

Mirlande explained the adoption process to the parents, and they agreed to put Islande and Jenica up for adoption if I would accept them. We started the preliminary process of obtaining legal birth certificates and having lab tests. Surprisingly, Islande's birth certificate had correct dates and names. Next, we went to the court to make a birth certificate for Jenica, and then took the mother and the girls for lab tests. Lab results usually take a week. When the results were delayed we feared bad news. Islande was HIV negative and all her other tests were fine. The mother, however, and baby Jenica tested HIV positive.

I had a 100 percent success rate in converting HIV **positive** babies to HIV **negative**, but we had to act quickly to convert Jenica to HIV negative. First we took the six-week old infant into our care and started her on formula so that she would not be infected by her mother's breast milk. We re-tested Jenica regularly, and fed her nutritious food with extra precaution to make sure she did not get sick, even sick with a cold. All of this was very important, as a baby only has 18 months to convert to negative or she will always be HIV positive.

Finding that the mother was HIV positive, however, presented a dilemma. Should we tell the father to get tested since his wife is HIV positive? This could bring many problems into their home, but if we did not tell him, more people could be infected, as marital fidelity is not a common practice in Haiti. We decided to tell the father, who was tested and pronounced HIV negative.

We told the father that his wife would infect him, and any sexual partners with this deadly disease. Did he even understand? Did he believe us? We did not know. I feared he would also get infected, and the children would eventually lose both parents.

Many believe that the majority of people in Haiti are infected with HIV, but **this is not true.** I test hundreds of people every year, most of whom are the very poorest, living from day to day hungry, sick, homeless, and unemployed. Jenica and her mother were the only HIV positive I found in 2011. I truly believe HIV is a much more common problem in the USA and other countries.

As for Jenica, she was a beautiful, happy baby. When we took her in, she never cried, so I needed to have someone special to care for her. The normal Haitian nanny will only feed and diaper a child when the child cries. I had several Americans take care of Jennica during their visits. Jenica would smile, and kick her legs to make her baby chair rock. It was quite remarkable how she would rock herself, and stay so happy. Jenica continued to test positive but her Western Blot gradually showed less positive. Finally, at age nine and a half months, Baby Jenica's test came back **negative**. All the prayers and good care had paid off.

The day after her first negative HIV test she was chosen for adoption. Praise God for his love and compassion on this beautiful child. Anyone could see she had no future in Haiti, other than pain and suffering. Her mother will eventually get sick and die, leaving the other three children motherless. As for the father, God only knows what will happen to him.

Baby Jenica overcame the deadly odds of converting from HIV positive to HIV negative and thus was crowned by Miss America Teresa Scanlan as our 2011 Reach Out to Haiti Princess. Jenica acted as if she knew exactly what her title meant. When someone asked, "Jenica, are you a princess?" she would lift her hand and smile like perfect royalty.

FELLOW MISSIONARIES, SANDRA AND JANE, HAVE DESCRIBED BARBARA AS:

B-bold
A-awesome
R-rebellious
B-butt kicking
A-amazing
R-Ruuska queen
A-authoritative / General

CHAPTER 14

Proverbs, Remedies, and Glossary

Haitian Proverbs

Haiti is a non-literate culture. 80% or more of the people neither read nor write. Consequently, wisdom is oral. There are no detailed philosophical systems in Haiti. People hand down their knowledge and express it in proverbs. In the rural areas hardly 5 or 6 sentences can pass in any serious conversation without someone throwing in a proverb as defense of some idea. There are hundreds of proverbs. (haitisurf.com)

1. A little dog is really brave in front of his master's house.
2. Roaches are never right when facing chickens.
3. Remember the rain that made your corn grow.
4. In times of famine, sweet potatoes have no skin.
5. Salt doesn't boast that it is salted.
6. Little by little the bird builds its nest.
7. The constitution is paper, bayonets are steel.
8. God is good.
9. Beyond the mountains, more mountains.
10. An empty sack can't stand up.

11. Speaking French doesn't mean you are smart.
12. If work were a good thing the rich would have grabbed it a long time ago.
13. Smelling good is expensive.
14. The rock in the water does not know the pain of the rock in the sun.
15. God says do your part and I'll do mine.
16. You know what you've got, but you don't know what's coming.
17. Wife for a time, mother for all time.
18. Past years are always better.
19. After the dance the drum is heavy.
20. A leaky house can fool the sun, but it can't fool the rain.
21. The giver of the blow forgets, the bearer of the scar remembers.
22. People talk and don't act.
23. God acts and doesn't talk.
24. If it is God who sends you, he'll pay your expenses.
25. Misfortune has no horn.

Remedies

One year I received five 2½ ton trucks full of medicine and medical supplies that we were able to distribute to more than 70 clinics and medical ministries. Among the items was a very large supply of suppositories. Since there wasn't a high demand for suppositories we developed a sales pitch that included **50 uses for suppositories.** Here are 25 of the best ideas.

1. Suppositories make great shoe polish. You'll get a good shine as well as renew natural moisture to the leather.
2. Suppositories can lubricate squeaky door hinges.
3. Suppositories can renew the shine to artificial plants.

4. Suppositories can ease the pain of sunburn. It's anti-inflammation ingredient will also reduce swelling.

5. Suppositories provide hand protection before painting or working with glue, tar, etc.

6. Suppositories help reduce swelling from insect bites.

7. Suppositories can lubricate and prevent rust in saws and other tools.

8. Suppositories can make it easier to work with dreadlocks.

9. Suppositories can be used to lubricate children's slides to provide a faster ride.

10. Suppositories are the nature lover's answer to furniture polish, and they won't destroy the ozone layer.

11. Suppositories can serve as auto polish.

12. Suppositories can help relieve pain and promote healing for small scrapes and abrasions.

13. Suppositories can prevent corrosion on battery terminals and help conduct current.

14. Don't lick flashlight or camera batteries to improve connection; just rub on a little suppository.

15. Apply a suppository to a handlebar mustache to keep it in place.

16. Having difficulty putting on or taking off tight fitting rings? Suppositories are the perfect answer.

17. Don't forget to rub a bit of suppository on keys to lubricate sticky locks.

18. Suppositories are great for animal lovers too. Just wipe one in your pet's ears to prevent ear mites or insect bites.

19. Do aluminum windows and screens stick when you try to open or close them? A suppository can make them slide easier.

20. Do you have newly pierced ears? Soothe the pain, promote healing and reduce swelling with our finest treatment. Suppositories are the answer.

21. How annoying it is to fight with your water hose when you try to put on that spray nozzle for watering flowers. Rub a little suppository on the threads of the nozzle and hose.
22. Rub a suppository on the fingers of children before they start finger-painting. Their fingers won't stain and they will create unique artistic paintings.
23. Suppositories are a truly low-cost way to reduce the puffiness under your eyes.
24. Parents! Need private time? Rub the doorknobs with suppositories so those small children can't open the door
25. When you experience that uncomfortable, unmentionable problem, you could actually use a suppository for its intended purpose.

Warning! Do not use suppositories for earplugs!!!

HELP WANTED

Are you looking for a career change?

Do you want a job that is **exciting, challenging,** inspiring and fulfilling?

Are you sick of doing the same mundane job day after day?

How would you like a job with flexible duties with **new** and **unusual tasks?**

A **"learn-as-you-go"** job where you can be compassionate, kind, inspiring, and loving?

Do you want to get away from the "yes sir" job and become a self-starting, independent worker, developing new projects and programs from your own ideas?

Are you searching for a job where you can set your own goals and see your accomplishments first hand, knowing that you made a real difference in someone's life?

Get away from that "separation of church and state" and get a career where God is the focus. Choose a job where you can **pray openly and seek God's guidance.**

Do you want to get away from the cold, snowy winters and work on a **good tan** instead of a **backache** from shoveling snow?

No more suit and ties or expensive dress codes for you. Casual and comfortable will be your new uniform.

Who wants to be stuck in a **stuffy office,** store, or factory all day?

Get out in the **fresh air**, meet **new people**, and **see places** that you could only read about!

Applications are being accepted now!

You can apply in person, by phone or by email. Forget the long and tedious resume. School and employment history are not important! Just have a pastor's reference or personal statement of Christian faith and call me to arrange an interview. It is really that simple. Stay for as long as God calls you!

RESPONSIBILITES

Include, but are certainly not limited to, **tour guide, recreation director, taxi,** meal preparation consultant, food pantry administrator, **medical diagnosis, EMT/nurse, pharmacist, minor pest control, maintenance, personal dispute mediator, education coordinator for small group studies, translator,** and **assorted clerical duties** involving **minor computer/typing, filing** skills.

WAGES/BENEFITS

Actual "**salary**" is based purely on voluntary donations that are offered by our clients on an intermittent schedule. **Room,** board, **meals,** all available **utilities** and **necessary personal care items** will be provided for you. Use of **cell** and **landline phone** services, **internet** access, and **generator** backup for electrical service interruptions, daily door to door water delivery and trash removal, **laundry** services and personal seamstress on site. **Resort/beach day** and overnight trips included on an intermittent schedule with frequent "**unscheduled" holidays.** Plenty of **open air markets** are available for your shopping convenience. Inexpensive and unique hand crafts and souvenir items available right outside your door (and almost everywhere else). Lots of sun, **warm** weather, gorgeous shoreline and ocean views.

This could be a **dream** job for the right candidate. Perhaps long term missions is not your style. Maybe consider coming for a week, month or even a summer. It is all up to you! Married couples, as well as their children are also welcomed. **Flexible scheduling** and **babysitting** services are available 24/7 with **live-in** playmates of all ages.

So, if you feel God calling you for a career with more opportunities than you could imagine, this is the perfect job for you! My door is always open and the phone is always on.

BARBARA'S GLOSSARY

25 ENGLISH WORDS WITH HAITIAN MEANINGS
With definitions and clarifications of meanings

1. **Exciting**—A chance to be a part of real-life Haiti drama. Sorry, no stand-ins for dangerous scenes.
2. **Flexible duties**—What shape pretzel can you form yourself into as you squeeze into a pick-up truck with 20 other people?
3. **Learn-as-you-go**—No training available
4. **Pray and seek God's guidance**—Should we take the road that takes two hours to get to town and is "safe" or the one that takes 15 minutes?
5. **Good tan**—You look like a cooked lobster.
6. **Memory**—Match the mother with the child. And don't forget the names, DOB, and complete story behind each one.
7. **Top Places to Visit**—Just because Haiti constantly makes the headline news, doesn't mean it's ranked among the top 10 places in the world to see.
8. **Tour guide**—"...and over on the left is **another** house belonging to our President ...
9. **Recreation director**—"Listen children, we don't write on the walls. And let's not play in the garbage. How about the swings? No, I didn't mean all of you on ONE swing!"
10. **Medical Diagnosis**—Easy to do since you, yourself, have already experienced scabies, e-coli, boils, parasites, anemia, impetigo, hepatitis, and ringworm.
11. **Pharmacist**—Person who dispenses pills and a dab of this or that on a piece of newspaper.
12. **Minor Pest Control**—Control of anything smaller than a goat: ants, cockroaches, tarantulas, rats, lizards, crickets, scorpions, mosquitoes, and fleas.

13. **Personal Dispute Mediator**—Someone experienced in handling a cat fight among women.

14. **Experiences**—Not everything in life should be experienced. Ask me about my experiences in 10 years, after I've finished therapy.

15. **Healthy prayer life**—"God, don't let them shoot us."

16. **Utilities in Haiti**: Electricity—always a pleasant surprise. Water—available to those who will pump. Plumbing—definitely a luxury.

17. **Bathing tips**—Pour clean water over your head. Lather well with soap. Pour more water over head. Step out of brown muddy puddle on the shower floor.

18. **Cell & landline phone**—A means of communication if the landline has not been cut or you can get a signal on your cell phone.

19. **Cyber cafes**—Avoid these dark, windowless, non-air-conditioned money holes. Pages take about five minutes to load and just when you are ready send or print, the generator quits, the computer screen goes black, and you are left in the dark.

20. **Generator**—When starting a generator, it is necessary to lay prayerful hands on it prior to starting and then duck for cover as you turn the knob.

21. **Laundry**—Clothes guaranteed to be spotless even if it means rubbing a hole in the fabric. Reshaping and stretching included. You may need suspenders for underwear.

22. **Unscheduled holidays**—Holidays observed when bridges and roads are blocked by demonstrators and fiery barricades.

23. **Open air markets**—A gathering place for dust-raising buses, flies, dogs, garbage and raw sewage.

24. **Warm**—Yes, Haiti is warm— as in "Hades" warm.

25. **Dream**—After being in Haiti a while, you **dream** of going home.

IT CAN'T GET WORSE

CHAPTER 15

Stormy Days

The Lord Giveth and the bandits taketh away

In 2006, Haiti had a presidential election and the results were questionable. The people were angry that corruption had once again marred the election. Most Haitians want fair and honest elections, but elections are repeatedly marked by corruption and fraud resulting in violence.

I had a visa appointment for Saulane and Maki and was excited to be taking two more children to their new families in the USA. All the plans had been made and airline tickets purchased for a Wednesday flight. Since Joe Hurston was in Haiti, he went with me to Port-au-Prince. We had gotten up early, loaded the truck with the children, nannies, and paperwork, and left for the city.

The roads were crammed with protesters. In a seven-mile stretch to the airport we encountered 20 roadblocks.

"Everything is going to be closed in Port," Joe said

"The consulate will definitely be closed," I replied. "We may as well turn around and head back home." We turned around at the airport and after talking our way through seven very difficult road blocks, we got back to the village.

Since we couldn't do Plan A on our schedule for the day, we turned to Plan B. We dropped off the children and caregivers at the village and picked up Johny and Mirlande to go to Mirebalais to deliver a water purifier. Joe got behind the wheel for the four-hour drive. When we reached the intersection of LiLavois and the Mirebalais road, we turned left and started up the road. Suddenly, a white pickup truck that looked like a police truck ran across the road and straight toward our front bumper. Joe had no choice but to stop.

Twelve to fourteen men, armed with rifles and hand guns and dressed in President Preval shirts jumped out and ran to our truck. They roughly pulled us from our truck and tried to force us into their truck. Joe and I refused, and fought them off because we knew they would hold foreigners for ransom.

Joe wore a vest and they were trying to get it off of him because they were sure he had money in the pockets. They would get one arm out and while they tried to pull his other arm out, Joe would quickly slip his other arm back into the vest. This went on like a game and baffled the thieves.

Meanwhile, I was fighting with two other men who were trying to get me into their truck. I kicked and punched them, which made them angry. Joe was concerned that they would shoot me and he reached over, grabbed me, and threw me to the ground. He said we have to pray. On our knees, he began to shout out to God. Our call for God's help frightened all the men around us. They looked like they saw a ghost or an army of angels. They ran to my truck and drove away with all the contents as well as all the money they had taken from us.

Robbery and kidnapping were happening way too often in Haiti. This had been my third escape from kidnappers. God spared Joe and me from being kidnapped and we suffered no major injuries, but our losses, were extensive. Joe lost his suitcase, computer, telephone, camera, about $4,000US cash and water purifiers. The Voyager water purifying systems were valued at $12,000US.

My losses were tragic. Not only did I lose a truck valued at $6,000US, but more devastating, I lost my briefcase containing the original documents and passport for Maki's visa. As I remembered all that had been in the briefcase, a sick feeling came over me. There were many important papers, photos and record books in the case. The original documents could be replaced, but it would require lots of money and time. Replacing the documents for Maki might take months and cause his American family to endure more delays.

Johny went in search for help and found two motorcycles and drivers to take Joe and me back to Ruuska Village. Johny and Mirlande stayed to try to retrieve some of our goods. For our safety, the drivers took us through the countryside, avoiding the roads. The route was so circuitous I wondered if Joe was thinking we had been kidnapped by the motorcycle drivers. As a precaution, I instructed the drivers to drop us at Johny's school. I never take strangers to my home. After dropping off passengers, some taxi drivers have returned to rob them.

Joe and I walked to the police department to report the attack. The police officers grabbed a mostly used paper to write down our information. After all there was still a 3" spot with no writing on the scrap of paper. Joe was not impressed by police report process.

Soon, a dozen or so of my village women arrived to help us. Then, to our surprise, Johny showed up with my truck. Praise God, the thieves gave it back. I can only think of two possible reasons why they returned the truck: the truck had a large sign on the side advertising "Nichols Brothers Boat Builders," the corner of which was pulled up. It looked like they tried to remove it with no luck. Or perhaps too many people recognized it was "Barbara's truck." I can't go anywhere in Haiti that people don't recognize my truck. I'm sure the people in the streets were asking, "What are **they** doing with Barbara's truck?"

We returned to the village and started calling our cell phone numbers. The bandits answered and Johny and Mirlande negotiated the return of some of our goods. After about ten phone calls, they agreed to return my briefcase for $600US and Joe's suitcase for $100US. Johny and Mirlande drove to meet with them and returned in about one hour. Our belongings had been dumped into the back of the truck. As we went through the pile, we found they had returned the valuable Voyagers, two of the cell phones, Joe's Bible and pictures of his wife and family, my blue dice that had hung from the rearview mirror of the truck and the photo copies of Maki's documents.

You just can't trust a thief! The agreement was for the return of my briefcase and Joe's suitcase but they hadn't been returned. Maki's original documents were in the briefcase. There was only one thing left to do — start the paperwork process for Maki's adoption again.

It can't get worse

I had been in Haiti for about 17 years and every year I would say that it can't get worse, but sure enough it did. February of 2004 came bringing increasing violence as several political groups fought for power. The people began to turn against President Aristide and demanded he leave office and Haiti. A select group of pro-Aristide warriors called the *chimere* (monsters) fought violently for Aristide —killing, burning and looting just about anything in their path. Death squads roamed the streets and a political gang culture ruled the slums of Citi Soleil.

Members of this group stopped Kindra and me and held guns to our heads. After a rather long discussion that I fondly call my "babbling idiot defense," they let us go. God was surely with us on that day. It brought to mind the old saying that "God protects the faithful and the foolish." I guess I qualified for both. When you face machine guns and 9mm hand guns all you can do is keep calm and trust in the Lord's plans.

Schools, businesses, and government offices had closed or were open on a random basis only. Prices skyrocketed and gasoline, diesel, and food supplies dwindled. Everyone needed rice but if you were lucky enough to find it you paid triple. Our work came to a standstill. With shooting in the streets and no gas no one traveled the streets. Electricity was shut down and people were hungry and angry.

Then came the biggest surprise of all. The *Tonton Macouts,* the old military personnel from the rule of the Duvaliers (Papa and Baby Doc) came out of hiding and began taking over the country. They came fast and with great force. "Remove Aristide!" they demanded. We watched and listened with amazement as the news reported city after city had been captured and support was growing as they progressed.

During that time, my daughter Colleen and her husband Tom and their daughter Amanda came to visit. Just days after they arrived the airports shut down, not to reopen for over a month. The US Embassy and Consulate closed and many officials were unable to leave the country. People were afraid to leave their houses. Barricades and burned out vehicles blocked most roads. Smoke rose from torched homes, vehicles, businesses, and government offices. Day and night, the sounds of gunfire ripped the silence of streets emptied of commerce.

So where were we during all of this? What were we doing? With businesses and offices closed, we could do no work so we embarked on a much needed vacation. Yes, you heard me right. We turned this chaos into quite an enjoyable time. After a good hard look at the situation I decided that since the rebels had already taken the northern towns, we should be able to travel rather safely to the northern beach resorts, which is exactly what we did. On nearly empty roads we drove along, leisurely taking photos of burned out police stations, banks, and cars. We chatted with a couple groups of friendly rebels and politely asked a group of pro-rebel supporters to move their road block so we could pass. Since the fighting in the north had halted we had an enjoyable ride out to resorts on the bay.

We stayed at one resort for two nights and were given a big discount and service to rival a five-star hotel. We were the only guests. After a couple days, we decided to try a new resort farther north. There we basked in quiet safety, swam, ate great food, and since we were the only guests, we again received royal treatment. That week, we were the only guests in all three resorts that we visited. From the safety of our hotel room we watched the news of Aristide's demise on TV.

After a very relaxing vacation, we returned to Port-au-Prince in hopes that my daughter and her family would be able to fly home. On the way to the airport, we passed massive destruction and the appearance of Canadian and US troops. Tanks, trucks and personnel vehicles of every size and type clogged the streets. Military planes and peace keepers swarmed the airport.

We asked a Canadian soldier if any planes were flying. "No," he said, "but if you have a US or Canadian passport you can go out on a military flight to the Dominican Republic. It will be leaving in about 45 minutes."

"How much would that cost?" I asked.

"Nothing."

What a deal! My daughter and her family made arrangements to leave on the military flight and were soon safely out of the country.

Later that night, my daughter called to taunt me. "After all your years in Haiti you were never flown out in a military evacuation, but we were."

In the Dominican Republic, American Airlines had honored their original tickets (flying from Haiti) with no extra charge and they had arrived home about two hours later than they had originally been scheduled to arrive. We still consider that our best vacation together.

Although Aristide had left and the UN patrolled the streets, the country was still in turmoil. Anger, unrest, riots, and war demonstrations kept life from returning to normal. Most schools stayed closed. People were suffering due to lack of work and necessities such as food and fuel for vehicles. We got up each day and tried to get some work done without putting ourselves into too much danger. Some businesses and government offices managed to open and those that had been burned out began to rebuild. Those were days when our faith—and a heavy dose of insanity—kept us in the country. During those troubled times we were still able to get visas so that 28 children could leave the country to start life in a safe, loving home.

As the political climate and violence started to ease up, however, along came the floods. In all my years here in Haiti, I have never seen so much rain. In September 2004 more than 2,500 people died when Tropical Storm Jeanne unleashed torrential rain on northeastern Haiti, triggering devastating floods and mudslides in Gonaïves. More floods followed in the fall. USAID said that 100,000 people had lost homes and were living in shelters.

As I have said many times, "It can't get worse." But it did. The next blow to Haiti exceeded everyone's wildest, most terrifying nightmare.

CHAPTER 16

January 12, 2010 4:53 PM

During this politically volatile time, Ruuska Village provided a safe haven for the women and children. The village gave the women security from the attacks on the street. All of our houses were filled with each lady taking in more relatives and friends. We had water and food and a large diesel-powered generator provided some power at the village.

In spite of the political turmoil, we continued to grow. Houses and gardens covered the property so the only way we could expand was by building on top of the current buildings. A kitchen and bath on top of House Number 2 was for visitors. A second floor on House Number 1 adjoined the second floor house on Number 2. This house provided a place for the babies and an apartment for Lawanna, an American lady who cared for the babies. Since schools were closed most of the time, and the streets weren't safe for children, we started a school at Ruuska to help the children with basic skills.

The unimaginable happens

During the 20 years I had spent in Haiti, I had handled riots, coups, hurricanes and floods but nothing could have prepared me for what happened on January 12, 2010. At 4:53 in the afternoon I was on the phone with Joe Hurston when the earth began to convulse.

No one will ever know the exact number of people who died in the earthquake, but government sources give a number of more than 230,000. Port-au-Prince, the capital, was decimated and surrounding towns and villages lay in rubble. Government buildings including the Presidential Palace fell. Homes and businesses, schools, and churches collapsed entombing people. Words and even pictures cannot describe the horror of the following hours and days. Bodies lined the streets. The smell of death hung in a thick pall over the city. As the earth continued to move, panic and fear overwhelmed the people and they ran erratically seeking safety.

God surely had a hand of protection over Ruuska Village. Around us, buildings fell killing our neighbors, but no one in Ruuska Village was hurt or killed. Some buildings suffered damage but buildings could be replaced. Aftershocks, sudden movements, or loud noise tormented and revived the terror of the quake. PTS (Post Traumatic Stress) reigned in the streets. Hundreds of thousands, of bleeding, crippled, hungry, thirsty, weeping people wandered through the rubble looking for family members. Some, not understanding the danger, went back into their homes for possessions or family members and died when aftershocks finished collapsing the houses. In the aftershocks, safety could only be found in open spaces away from still crumbling, walls and buildings.

At Ruuska Village, we moved out of the houses and into the yard. The babies cried and cried. There was so much to do and so many to care for and not enough people to hold and comfort the babies. Desperation and confusion were everywhere

The immediate and terrifying needs of the city were overwhelming. The airport and shipping port were closed due to the destruction and it seemed no medical or basic needs could be meet. Joe Hurston, though, was able to fly in with relief supplies the next day. We put the children in tents and soon our village became a tent shelter for our neighbors.

For weeks we worked nonstop just to get and provide additional necessities such as food, water, and basic medical care amidst the chaos all around us. God's hand, however, was evident in every step, every hour, and in every part of the process. Unbelievably, at the time of the quake, we had just received a month's worth of food and we had two registered nurses visiting with us. I had just purchased food only days before the quake. Our food depot was full. It was like God had me prepare in time.

We were housing and feeding hundreds of people a day. We had food to share, plenty of medical supplies and many slept in or near the village. The darkness in the cities and villages was more frightening to the people than usual but our generator provided some light which gave the people comfort.

Women of Ruuska work together

The women at Ruuska united as a family and helped each other search for family members that were lost in the city. I was so proud of my women, as I watched them reach out to help and comfort their friends, neighbors, and families. They united in prayer for the injured and the missing people. They went out searching for survivors and brought the injured back for treatment. They welcomed people into the village for medical treatment, food, and a safe place to sleep.

Again, food, gas and diesel were very difficult to get. Our women went out into the streets to find supplies. The "hunting" expeditions sometimes turned up prize bananas, watermelons and potatoes that had been brought in from outlying areas unaffected by the quake. The women's commitment to help others touched me and made me feel that all the years of frustration in training them to take responsibility had been worthwhile.

Our clinic had not been damaged and again I saw how God had prepared us for this tragedy. The clinic was fully stocked with the meds and supplies and the two nurses who had been at Ruuska Village stayed to treat the wounded. During and after the earthquake water-borne disease killed many. Our water purification units worked over time to provide safe drinking water to thousands of people.

They came all day long to fill their jugs and bottles with pure water and also get food. God continued to bless us with workers and donations. People from all over the world reached out to help, enabling us to be a small rescue center for our neighbors. We handed out tents, tarps, bedding, clothing, food and medicine. The earthquake brought horrifying tragedy, but at the same time, immeasurable opportunities to bless others.

Getting the little ones to safe places

Volunteers and the women of Ruuska Village kept the relief effort flowing while I worked to get children out of the country. Scores had been in the adoption pipeline and families in several countries frantically called to see if **their** children were safe. Parents were concerned about their children and wanted to rush them out of danger to safety. Joe Hurston and I spent day after day, some days 15 hours, in the American Consulate applying for Humanitarian Paroles for our children. Donated planes came in to take our children to safety in the USA. Argentina and Canada gave humanitarian visa's to children being adopted in their countries. During all this tragedy, desperation and confusion, 86 children left Haiti from Ruuska Village to find safety with loving families.

One story will give you an idea of what one family went through during that turbulent time to finish the adoption process for their little girl.

Due to the earthquake, we were unable to finish the adoption in the usual manner. We petitioned for the USCIS to grant our child entrance into the United States as a refugee on Humanitarian Parole. Upon the Haitian Prime Minister's approval for her to leave Haiti, we were notified that Barbara would escort our baby girl and an older boy to Miami in 2 days! We threw luggage in the car and starting driving to Florida, on what we called our "big adventure." Our baby girl was really coming!

At Miami International Airport, we waited anxiously for the afternoon flight from Haiti. Travelers came and went, but there was no sign of Barbara and two children. Concerned, we made a few phone calls. Ruska Village confirmed they were on their way.

After being delayed in Haiti, which resulted in missing their scheduled flight, they had taken a later flight that would arrive around 8:00 p.m. The plane arrived on schedule, but still we waited and waited. Another couple, with their two young children, were there to greet their adopted son who was the boy coming with Barbara.

The arrival area emptied and janitors came through sweeping the floors. There was still no sign of Barbara and the children. Finally, at 1:00 a.m. a weary Barbara came through the doors carrying our daughter. An adolescent boy was at her side. US Customs officials had made them sit and wait and processed them last. We were able to hold our daughter for a short time, then she and the boy were escorted to a children's home for processing.

The next morning we went through the processing of documents with the Department of Homeland Security. Upon completion, they released her to us. She was 18 months old and adorable. She captured the hearts of all who saw her. We then finished the remaining adoption process here in the USA.

Initially we spent all of our energy just sustaining basic needs but soon we were able to start looking at the big picture and the rebuilding process. When the aftershocks finally abated, engineers assessed the damages to Ruuska Village and decided which buildings were stable, which ones could be repaired, and which ones needed torn down and replaced. Architects and engineers donated their time to render blueprints for new buildings and infrastructure that would meet the highest building standards of a developed country. Buildings were designed to withstand hurricanes and quakes and be a viable and safe home for orphans for many years to come.

CHAPTER 17

A Repairer of Broken Walls

… you will be called Repairer of Broken Walls,
Restorer of Streets with Dwellings. (Isaiah 58:12)

Donations of money and goods started coming. Mandi, one of the nurses who had been helping at Ruuska, went home to raise money and donations. She and her husband's company were able to send cargo containers of building supplies, tools, food and baby supplies into Haiti. A Florida fund-raising project called India Fest raised a super large amount to aid the rebuilding efforts. It was as if everyone I had ever met started raising funds for Ruuska Village. My head was spinning with delight and my heart overflowed with gratitude. There is no way to describe how wonderful it felt to see that people believed in the work I was doing in Haiti and wanted to help rebuild the village.

Can I go home now?

To be honest, I had considered quitting and going home to a comfortable retirement. After all, I was now 66 years old and had worked more than 20 years in Haiti. I had fought a good fight, lived in poverty in a hot, dirty, garbage-filled country, helped women and babies find a better life and even been kidnapped and assaulted. Now, in spite of all my work I was watching Haiti literally die before my eyes. Haiti was hopeless.

Then I came to my senses. I knew that was not true. Yes, without God, Haiti is hopeless. Tragedy fills the country because the people serve Voodoo gods that promote selfishness. Until the people wholeheartedly turn to God, heartache, sadness, depression and death will fill their future. With God though, Haiti could be a country filled with hope.

I did not go home. The overwhelming support, love and encouragement gave me reason to stay and the reconstruction of Ruuska Village began. When the protective walls went back up, razor wire topped them. In spite of all that we had **given** to neighbors, thieves had started breaking into our depots. After the front wall and gate received a face lift, we began tearing down buildings that would have to be rebuilt. The food depot and tool depot were enlarged. Another floor was added to House #4, and an addition on House #5 allowed me to move my bed out of the office and have my first private space with a small bath. The painters even used my favorite color – blue.

Once again, we were safe in Ruuska Village but I watched sadly as desperation and crime increased. Eleven months after the quake only 5% of the rubble had been removed from the streets and city lots. Six hundred thousand (600,000) people still lived in tent cities, many with no toilets, water supply or power. The tents held all of their possessions and left them vulnerable to thieves and storms. As the tarps and tents disintegrated from the heat of the sun and wind, the people scrounged through the rubble in search of "new walls" for their shelters.

Without access to safe water, malaria and typhoid were rampant. When Nepalese peacekeepers introduced cholera to Haiti, nearly a half million people contracted the disease. More than 6,000 died. Although relief agencies and governments boasted of all the help they had sent to Haiti, there was no sign that Haiti would ever get better.

Our ladies had continued to welcome friends and family to stay with them. Before long our houses were overcrowded. We needed more houses. Funds came in to rebuild and grow, but our **land was too small** to meet the increasing need for homes.

Survival comes before hope

I really had no intention to expand Reach Out to Haiti, but when you see devastation and desperation you can't help but do all that you can to help as many as you can. My goal with Reach Out to Haiti and Ruuska Village had been to help a **small group** of women, by providing long term assistance and education. I wanted to mentor and instill in them the hope for a better life and brighter future which would enable them to become better mothers.

The earthquake, though, had damaged so many families. It had taken away their homes and possessions, but most of all it had taken away all hope. They had buried their dead, and started over, plagued by fear, sadness, depression, and sometimes, anger. With all that they had lost it was difficult to think about the future. They didn't need education, mentoring, or goals for a bright future. They needed food and shelter from predators and the elements.

I was able to buy a house next door to the village that had escaped major damage in the quake. We called the house "Doctor Charles's House." The house had three large bedrooms, a kitchen and a room large enough to serve as a fellowship hall. Visitors and volunteers who needed accommodations would be able to stay there and we could use the former guest accommodations in the village to house more homeless women.

Maki Island

Money poured in from so, so many people in the USA, Argentina, Canada and Germany. Astrid, a German dentist, who had adopted two children from Haiti and was in the process of adopting two more, set out to raise funds for the increasing demand for housing. She was ambitious and determined to show the German people how they could help. She solicited donations from friends, family, the German Dental Association, The Lions Club Rhede, and adoption agencies to build "Maki Island." The name was appropriate because the land as well as the adjoining parcels of land was a big swamp. Just as in Ruuska Village, we built the houses on raised footings above the land. We brought in truckloads of fill which created the island effect. Maki was a dry island-refuge in a swamp.

The earthquake destroyed so much and created such a huge demand for building supplies that everything cost nearly double the previous price. On Maki Island, though, we had funds to build three homes for women and children who were not up for adoption. Additionally, we had two storage containers, bathrooms, shower rooms, a well, and one solar light to provide light all night.

THE OTHER SIDE
OF ADOPTION

CHAPTER 18

Certificate of Occupancy

One of the great joys of my work is completing the adoption process and placing a child in the arms of the adopting parents. Sometimes a parent or parents come to Haiti for the child. Other times I take the child to the parents.

The first recorded adoption

On this day, I'm on an American Airline flight to take two boys to their new parents. As I sit here I look over at the boys. Excited and nervous they are looking around in wonder and surely feeling a bit frightened. They have put on the headphones, but I don't know if they are tuned to music or not. James, the older of the two is fingering through a book he didn't want to leave behind in Haiti. I point to the page he has open with a picture of baby Moses in a basket on the water.

"*Moyiz* (Moses)" I say. "Moses was adopted just like you." It was probably the **first recorded adoption** in history.

When food is served James is too nervous to eat, but saves his chocolate for another time. Nehemiah eats his whole meal and the extra chocolate the steward gave him. When we land and exit,

James leads the way to immigration. I'm sure he is just following the crowd, but he looks like he knows where we are going.

When we reach escalators, I prepare to grab James' hand and show him how to maneuver the steps, but he bravely steps on and breaks out in a big smile. Nehemiah follows with a bit of a balance problem. They both look at me and grin ear to ear in amazement. Now that they have mastered moving stairs their eyes get big as the room (transit car) we have entered starts to move. They are staring at the people around us. After living in a country of 95% black people, their eyes focus on the many white people around us. We spend 2 ½ hours in immigration and they still seem mesmerized by all the people coming and going.

Beyond the gates of immigration I will release them into the hands of a waiting family. I've done all that I can do to put them into a loving Christian family. They will enter a world of possibilities that they never could have experienced in Haiti. My prayer is that they will follow God and take advantage of all that is provided for them.

Babies for cats—and a few dogs too

Many people contact me for information on adoptions. The number one question is, "How much will it cost?" Then comes the next question. "I would love to adopt, but how could I ever find that kind of money?"

I tell them, "If God wants you to adopt, the money will show up, but you may have to use your imagination and do some fund raising."

Donna is a single woman in Washington State who found a creative way to fund not only one, but five adoptions. I met Donna in 1998 when she came to Haiti to pick up her first Haitian child, a little boy.

Donna, a happy, cheerful, and confident person with a strong personality was certain of what she wanted in life and that included children—lots of children. She worked as a nurse and had already adopted a little girl from China. After spending time with Donna I recognized that we were of kindred spirits. We enjoyed talking and even laughing about the problems of living in Haiti. She obtained the necessary visa for the child and they returned to the US.

Not long afterward she called telling me about the joy the young boy had brought to her life, and she felt God was providing a way for her to adopt again. On July 4, 2000, I was able to travel to Washington to take her a little girl. Every year I nominate a child from the village to be named my princess and she was my princess for the year 2000. Not only was she intelligent and beautiful, she was a real pleasure to care for.

I stayed as a guest in Donna's home for a few days and noticed that the house was set up for the safety and pleasure of the children. One thing that caught my attention was a big chain attached to her floor lamp and screwed into the wall.

"I see you have the lamp chained," I said. "Does the lamp get wild at times?"

She laughed and said, "I don't want the lamp to fall and hurt one of the children."

I couldn't help but ask, "Why are there large eye bolts in the wall?"

"Those are for a hammock," she said. "The children love to swing in a hammock."

Always mindful of the children's welfare, I asked more questions. "I notice you seem to get a lot of phone calls."

"Oh, those calls are for kittens. People are calling to buy kittens."

This woman was a nurse, had adopted three children and was raising cats? I had to ask, "So you raise cats?"

"I don't raise cats," she said. "I get them free from local farms, feed stores, and advertisements." She went on to explain. "I bathe them, give them their shots, put a flea collar on them, and let the children play with them and get them used to being with people. Then I place an ad in the newspaper and sell them for $50 to $75 each."

"What!" I said. I was astonished, "Mutt kittens! Who is crazy enough to buy them at that price?"

She looked at me with a joy in her eyes and replied "Lots of people. How do you think I get the money to adopt my children? I sell kittens!" Washington is full of *Yuppies*. They think if it costs money they need it and have to have it."

I thought, "She must be kidding." Then she pulled out the newspaper so I could read the ad. I giggled aloud as I read: **Free Kittens, Free Kittens**. There were about 15 different ads for free kittens. Then I read Donna's ad: **Kittens $ 75.00 each**.

She explained, "My first ad listed the price at $50 but the kittens sold so fast I ran out of kittens. I had to raise the price to $75 to keep up with the demand."

"These people come," she said, "with photos of their homes, fenced in backyards, letters from vets assuring that the kittens will be spayed and neutered as well as finishing a series of vaccinations, and letters from landlords stating they have no objection to the kitten adoption."

She would ask the adoptee several questions and then suggest a cat food. After paying $75 the new owner would leave with a squirming little bundle of joy and as the door shut Donna would say to herself. "I'm getting a new baby with this money!"

As long as there are children who need a good home and God provides the means for Donna to adopt, she will bring more children into her home, but she continues to use creative financing. In order to adopt a fourth child, she decided to expand her business to include puppies. She gathers free, unwanted puppies and she and the children prepare them for adoption. She gets $125 per pup, except for blonde color puppies. They cost $150.

When I brought a little boy to join her family I said, "Two girls, and two boys. Is your family complete now?"

"No," she said, "there are still more children who need a good home."

CHAPTER 19

Why Adopt?

Why do people adopt? Why make such a difficult and permanent decision? One mother describes how she and her husband came to the decision to adopt Carolane.

Carolane's story

In May of 2004, my husband and I started feeling the Lord speaking to us about adopting again. We had been blessed with the adoption of twins in 2001. We began to pray separately about the adoption. We really felt led to adopt an older child. Barbara had her heart set on us adopting the cutest little baby boy, but God had an even BIGGER plan. Barbara sent us a packet of pictures of children that were waiting for their forever families. One afternoon, I entered the kitchen and saw the twins were sitting on the stairs looking at the packet. I sat down with them to see what they were thinking. They began to ask me questions about the little girl they found in the packet. It wasn't a baby, or even a three year old, it was a seven-year-old little girl. They wanted to know why she looked so sad and if she had a mommy and daddy. I did not know her story at that time, so I told them that her parents probably could not take care of her, so she lived in the village. They instantly said, "Wait, can't you be her mommy and daddy be her daddy?" Instantly I knew that God was reaffirming the call He gave to us to adopt an older child.

It took us until December 23ʳᵈ that year to bring our beautiful girl home. She was seven by then. Carolane Olivia was the best Christmas present we could ever have gotten in 2004. The fact that they signed her papers in time for us to be home for Christmas was a miracle. She is the "poster child" for adoption. The only issues Carolane has ever shown is her struggle to always be independent. She remembers many things about Haiti, because she was seven when she came to live with us. She quickly acclimated to our family. She was the missing puzzle piece.

The story does not end there. The baby that Barbara wanted us to adopt not only lives down the road from us, but our Carolane had helped take care of him when he was born. God's amazing plans are so much bigger than ours.

Carolane has always loved Haiti and she continues to love it at the age of 17. She has returned with our church youth group to do VBS and other ministries in Ruuska Village twice since we have adopted her. The most amazing "God Plan" is that she plans to return to Haiti to serve the Lord when she graduates. She answered the call to serve last year while attending Bible camp. Our prayer for her is that she focuses on what God wants her to do. We all must remember that our children are borrowed from God for a short time, and we must allow Him to guide them in the way He sees is best for them.

Adoption isn't easy

One father wrote,

My wife and I adopted two children, ages nearly 4 and 5 from Haiti via Reach Out to Haiti in 2007. They are now 11 and 12 and settled into family life very well with us.

The adoption process is a long and agonizing one, with uncertainty throughout. It's not much fun, but it is hugely rewarding. It's hard to imagine the process working without the dedication, expertise and perseverance of Barbara Walker and Reach Out to Haiti. We made two trips to Haiti as part of the process so we saw first-hand the complexities and multiple hurdles to clear.

It would be so, so good if somehow the world would understand the huge benefits of adoption and make the process much easier.

Finding a way out after the quake

Words cannot express our gratitude to you for all you have done, especially camping out at the embassy those two days plus in order to get visas for Lovelie and Wisken when you had so much devastation to deal with at your village. We cannot begin to imagine what you have been through the past weeks and what you will deal with in the months and years ahead....Thank you for how you have blessed our family. We are truly grateful.

From Buenas Aires, Argentina

Genia and Andrice are very good (are fine) and have grown a lot. Andrice has completed the first year of primary school and is very happy to read a book without help. He wants to be an inventor and paleontologist (he likes dinosaurs).

Genia has finished nursery school and will go to primary school next year. She wants to be a painter and learn to dance ballet. They are very intelligent, curious, and naughty and are good sweet and loving.

We send you a kiss and a hug.

An observer says ...

Barbara is a very caring and grounded woman who is not afraid to demonstrate tough love when it comes to saving a soul. And when she takes a child in her arms and says "I'm gonna get you a Mommy and Daddy!" you can rest assured that with the glory and grace of the Lord her word is bond.

Typical newsletters

I receive many e-mails, cards, and letters that sound like typical newsletters American (North and South) families send out on holidays. The children are advancing through school, have a new puppy, have medals in track, love to dance, have artistic talent, play basketball, are active in church youth group, love to babysit, have a grass mowing business, works part-time at a store, is checking out college scholarships and now the older ones are sending wedding invitations.

BUT, you are destroying their culture

One of the biggest complaints I hear regarding adoptions, is that we will destroy the child's culture. I tell them that they may be right about the bad side of the culture. I strongly come back with this comment: "Yes, they will not have eight sexual partners before they reach their teens. They will not be a slave to Voodoo beliefs. They will not choose to beg in the streets rather than getting a job. They will not be using the streets as toilets and garbage disposals. They will not have to lie, cheat, and steal to survive. They will not die from simple curable conditions like diarrhea, dehydration, or childhood ailments such as measles, mumps, or fevers. On the other side, they will continue the Haitian culture of music, art, and sports. They will be able to excel in the positive aspects of the Haitian culture because they will be healthy and strong."

CHAPTER 20

Sometimes You Win. Sometimes You Don't.

Sometimes, no matter how hard you try and pray, how much you provide, how much you encourage, some women do not want to escape the unending, spinning cycle of desperation. At some point, those who want most to help these women become enablers who help perpetuate a begging lifestyle. The more you do for them, the more they ask for. Nothing is ever enough. Gratitude never comes. They destroy their blessings by always asking for more and more until the person helping must say, "NO!" The women reject the love that the giver meant to show and turn anger, resentment and blame on their benefactor.

Accencia

I first met Accencia in 2001 when she came to me with her first daughter, Kencia who was a down-syndrome child. I was able to get the child a medical visa to go to the USA for treatment and physical therapy. Even though Kencia has limitations she was eventually adopted and is living a good life in the USA.

Accencia was always a pleasant person. I enjoyed helping and encouraging her. I had hopes she would learn to take responsibility for herself and her future children. I was hoping she would learn to thank God for her blessings and become a grateful, content woman. I see now these were my hopes and dreams, not hers.

Usually, the unwed mothers at the village change their attitude toward life when they get documents of identity, so I tried to build Accencia's self-esteem by getting a birth certificate and identification card. Unfortunately, I saw no sign of progress or responsibility in Accencia. On December 29, 2004, she gave birth to Mackenley Joseph. Again, this child was fathered by a man who had no intentions of providing a life for Accencia or the child. Accencia continued moving from man to man, house to house. She was not willing to help herself.

I even purchased a house for her, but she soon walked away from that and left her son, with her sister. No matter how likeable Accencia was, she just could not get her life together. After having another child, that was adopted by a family in Argentina, she came to Ruuska Village for a while. She had a good life at Ruuska and a good steady income doing laundry, but then she wanted to move to Maki Island. At Maki Island she came up with the great idea that I could help her build a house near Cité Soleil. I told her she could save money to build the house. At the same time she was begging for help to build the house, she quit her job doing laundry. That was the end of my desire to help Accencia.

Spreading disease

IBESR, the Social Services for Haitian children, called us November 9, 2013, asking us to take in Jessica, a sixteen-year old girl and her newborn baby that she wanted to give up for adoption.

The sick, malnourished girl arrived in our village on November 10, 2013, with her two month premature baby boy, who weighed less than three pounds. The first thing we did was to set her up in a house in Ruuska Village and then get them to a doctor. I insisted on her staying with her baby until we could complete lab tests and obtain the proper documents needed.

A social worker interviewed the mother and a psychologist examined the child. The mother reported to the social worker that she lived on the streets of Cité Solei and did not want to keep the baby nor did she want to live in Ruuska Village. She said she wanted to return to the streets where she was free to do what she wanted to do. We had to watch her very carefully so she would not run away from the situation before we got the lab results back.

The mother signed all of the required papers of abandonment for the baby and stayed until the test results were in. It turned out that the mother was HIV positive and as if that wasn't enough, she also had syphilis. Jessica refused to stay after she was told the results of her lab tests, and went back to the streets to spread the disease. She would not even accept treatment for syphilis.

We named this sweet baby boy Ryan Charles and started him on antibiotics for the syphilis the mother had passed to him. In addition, we started him on my special vitamin and nutrition program to help him reject this HIV virus. We placed Ryan in the care of Nelta Pierre, our best nanny, who often cared for our premature and HIV babies. After several months of loving care Ryan tested negative for both syphilis and HIV. As for Jessica, the last I knew, she was extremely ill and suffering from the poor choices she had made throughout her life.

PERSPECTIVES

From Where I Saw It

He has made everything beautiful in its time. He has also set eternity in the human heart; yet no one can fathom what God has done from beginning to end. (Ecclesiastes 3:11)

CHAPTER 21

I Love Haiti.
I Love It Not.

Haiti was once called the Garden of Eden and the Pearl of the Antilles. Now it is the poorest and one of the most barren countries in the Western Hemisphere. People live in Haiti without even the essentials of life – water, food and shelter. How did this happen? Economists and politicians have their answers but I believe Haiti's choice of gods has brought them to this point of despair.

The saying goes that "Haiti is 85% Catholic; 15% Protestant; 100% Voodoo." God's Word says "Thou shalt have no other gods before me." God does not share worship with any other gods and I do not believe God will bless Haiti until the people acknowledge God as the one true God. We are instructed to worship him and only him.

It is very difficult to live in Haiti, but it has many rewards and blessings. My life in Haiti is definitely a love/hate relationship and I've expressed it in the following way.

I WILL CONTINUE BECAUSE THE
CHILDREN NEED ME.

My body is old, tired and weak,
longing for an easier life.
BUT I WILL CONTINUE BECAUSE
THE CHILDREN NEED ME.
I hate the hot temperature.
I love that we don't have five feet of snow, as in New York.
I hate the sound of gun fire and dogs barking at night.
I love that I have walls and weapons for protection.
I hate the corrupt government.
I love the BLUE police cars!
I hate that the American Consulate would
let a child die rather than be adopted.
I love seeing the excitement of an adopting parent
meeting their child for the first time.
BUT I WILL CONTINUE BECAUSE
THE CHILDREN NEED ME.

I hate seeing dead people lying on the streets.
I love that God brought me to Haiti to save many.
I hate being denied a medical visa
for a child that needs care.
I love that we have at least been granted a few visas.
I hate seeing children hungry.
I love that we can give food to hundreds of families.
I hate that the main food in Haiti is beans and rice.
I love that Haiti has the BEST bottled Coca Cola in the world!
I hate that the men go from woman to woman,
spreading their seeds, only to deny the child later.
I love seeing adoptive fathers caring for the babies.
I hate that desperate women must sleep around for food.
I love that our village women don't have to anymore.

BUT I WILL CONTINUE BECAUSE
THE CHILDREN NEED ME.

I hate that it is not safe to let my guests walk the streets.
I love meeting volunteers that come to help at the village.
I hate that one in five babies die before the age of five.
I love that I can save some.
I hate garbage thrown everywhere.
I love that Haiti has started to recycle.
BUT I WILL CONTINUE BECAUSE
THE CHILDREN NEED ME

I hate that educated men can only do white-collar work.
I love seeing women learn to read and make saleable crafts.
I hate that bad roads make me buy
new tires every six months.
I love driving on paved roads when I'm back in the USA.
I hate seeing NO hope of a bright
future for the children in Haiti.
I love success stories from children that have been adopted.
I hate searching for the bit of truth
among all the lies I am told.
I love that God gave me common sense and discernment.
I hate telling visitors, "DO NOT
WASTE, water, food, electricity.
I love to see visitors go home and teach others "Do Not Waste."
I hate hearing children cry.
I love yelling, "Make that baby happy!"
I WILL CONTINUE BECAUSE THE
CHILDREN NEED ME.

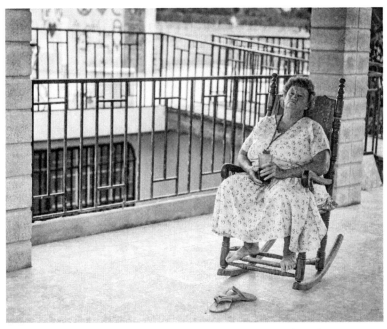

Be with you as soon as I finish my cold Coke.
Photography by audreydewys.com

CHAPTER 22

"Please, Give My Baby Life."

No matter how hard we try, how much we sacrifice, how much we give and encourage, often our efforts seem not to make a difference. Sometimes, though, after years of frustrating setbacks, we see responsibility begin to emerge in a mother and we watch in awe at how God transforms her life, how the Holy Spirit whispers to someone in another country about adoption, and how a child finds hope in a new family but still embraces his birth family. The characters in this true story are Barbara, Mirlande, Maggie, Matthew (Julio), and Old Joseph.

BARBARA

Mirlande is the daughter of Clariciar Antone and Gexeme Joseph. Her parents were married and had two girls and two boys together. Mirlande was five years old when her father died. Her mother sent her to live with a friend of her father where she lived with the family and did housework. She did not go to school, just learned how to clean, cook, and wash clothes. This man was not very nice to Mirlande. She was then sent back to live with her biological mother, who had remarried and had another baby girl. The baby girl died at the age of five. Mirlande's mother got pregnant, yet again, but this time both the child and mother died during labor. When the mother died, Mirlande, her brother Alterson, and her sister Tan Tan each went to live with different families.

The father's cousin soon came to get Mirlande, saying she could live with him and attend school. With this in mind, Mirlande went to live with him. However, to no surprise, she was not sent to school. He did put his three other children in school, but not Mirlande. She ended up as a house maid for them for three years. They were extremely cruel to her.

MIRLANDE

My mother and father died when I was just a young girl. I was passed around from family to family to work for my food. One family truly cared for me, but, they did not send me to school as they did their biological children.

BARBARA

At age eighteen, Mirlande moved with a friend to Warf Jeremie, a very poor village on the ocean. She got pregnant right away and gave birth to a baby girl named Nana. Nana's father had another wife and was of no financial help raising the baby. By age two, Nana was suffering from malnutrition, dehydration, and diarrhea. Mirlande took her to the General hospital, but they would not care for her because Mirlande did not have the 100 gourds ($2 USD) to pay the hospital fees. Baby Nana died.

Soon Mirlande met another man, Michellet Francois. They rented a small shack where he and Mirlande lived together. She was soon pregnant with her second child. Julio was born on December 7th, 1998.

MIRLANDE

I gave birth to my second child, Julio Francois, alone in Cité Solei His father, Michelet Francois, was in jail at the time. With no help, I went to the grandfather Old Joseph (as we respectfully called him).

"Michellet is in jail," I told him. "The baby is sick and I have no one to help me. I don't want this baby to die like my last one did."

Old Joseph said, "I cannot help you but Barbara Walker might help you. She helped me when I needed help." Old Joseph and his three children, twins Michellet and Fignole and a girl named Baby, had been one of the first families Barbara Walker had helped when she first came to Haiti in 1988.

Joseph's wife had left Haiti to live a better life in the USA, but she had left the children for Joseph to raise by himself. Old Joseph sold art and craft souvenirs at the gate of the Ormiso, where Barbara lived and worked for almost 10 years. He made enough money to feed the children, but needed help to send them to school. Barbara made a birth certificate for Baby, she was just called Baby because so many babies die that they wait until the child needs to go to school before they make the birth certificate. For years Barbara paid for tuition, books, and uniforms for the children. As time went by, the boys left home, but Old Joseph still needed help with Baby. Barbara, now a dear friend, had continued to help him. Old Joseph told me, "Barbara is accepting children for adoption. Let me take the baby to her."

BARBARA

When Old Joseph brought Julio to me the baby was very small, sick and had reddish hair that signaled malnutrition with a serious lack of iron and protein in his diet.

"Old Joseph," I said, "I can't take the baby unless both the mother and father come to sign for the adoption."

MIRLANDE

I went to the jail to get the father out so we could sign the papers. All we asked for was "**Give our Baby life**."

MAGGIE

Adoption was not something Mark and I had discussed prior to getting married over 25 years ago. We had 2 biological daughters ages 2 and 4 and had planned to have more children but hadn't discussed much more than that.

I was attending a Bible study at the time and another Mom in our group would come to the study with what seemed to be a different group of kids each week, different colors and ages and I was immediately drawn to her unique family. One day she told our group her story. She and her husband had heard about the orphan crisis in America and around the world and were compelled to do something about it. They had begun to foster several children in their home. This Mom shared the challenges and joys they had experienced since they entered this journey and looked each of us in the eye and said "you all can be part of the solution."

My heart nearly leapt out of my chest and I couldn't think of another thing for the rest of the day. When Mark came home from work that night, our journey began. I told him I was convinced that we needed to explore this avenue called adoption and he was up for learning more. Our first adoption was our son Marcus. He came from a nearby city and was full African-American. Our counselor at the time told us that if we were open to bringing a child of color into our white family that we needed to adopt more than one, so Marcus wasn't alone.

Marcus was one month old when he came into our family, our daughters were three and five at the time. Almost as soon as Marcus came into our home, we started the process of adopting again. We were open to domestic adoption again, however, God had been pulling at our hearts to explore international adoption. We were open to this and found Barbara Walker from Reach out to Haiti.

We were immediately drawn to Barbara as we poured over her adoption packet and stories that were included. She was the real deal, no bells and whistles, just a woman with a huge heart who desired a better life for some of the poorest of the poor on our planet. …We made the decision to pursue our next adoption through Barbara and her Reach out to Haiti ministry. Back in the early 90's adoption from Haiti was relatively easy.

We identified our son Matthew from a list of babies that Barbara had available for adoption. We didn't want to see photos so we just told Barbara to choose the youngest baby. This would be our son Matthew. Matthew's birth name was Julio Francois and his birth mom was Mirlande. Mirlande at the time was living on the street with no job, no money and a baby she couldn't care for.

Mark and I arrived in Port-au-Prince in April of 1999. We met Mirlande and Julio at the airport, as well as his birth father Michellet. We spent the week getting to know our new son, and the country that he came from. It was our first trip to Haiti and Barbara took us all around the city. We visited the foster homes where Barbara hired Haitian families to care for the orphans ready for adoption. (This was before Ruuska Village was built.) We spent our days visiting babies in homes and delivering the weekly formula, diapers and food for their care.

MATTHEW JULIO

I was named Julio Francois by my parents Mirlande Joseph and Michellet Francois. My birth parents never married and are currently not even in day to day contact. At the age of five months I was adopted by Mark and Maggie Mohr and brought into their loving, caring home in America. Although too young to remember my short time living in Haiti; I know I lived with Michellet during the day but ended up with Mirlande during the nights. My story is a very stereotypical Haitian adoption story. I was very sick and malnourished due to that fact that I was a starving baby living on the streets. I was very close to death but was fortunate enough to find someone who would help us. My grandpa Joseph knew of a woman named Barbara Walker and took me and my mother to her and asked her to help us which she did. That is the greatest gesture I have received to this day. For to this day I know Mirlande had me adopted so I could have a better life than she had.

BARBARA

It wasn't long before Mirlande was pregnant, yet again. I brought her to Bon Repos to live with me. Mirlande did some cooking, cleaning, and came to the city every day to help me. Her English started to improve and I taught her how to play Yahtzee to learn her numbers. She was a fast learner.

MAGGIE

Before we departed for home with our new son Julio we learned that Mirlande was pregnant with another boy. Her wishes were that we'd adopt him as well. We made plans to return to Haiti soon to bring home another son, Maki.

BARBARA

Maki was born on December 19, 1999, and adopted to the same family that had adopted Mirlande's son Julio. Julio's name had been changed to Matthew. He was now one year old.

I rented a house for Mirlande in Croix-des-Bouquets, but she did not like it there. I then rented her a house in Bon Repos, where she met a man named Pierre Jean from the Dominican Republic. She soon got pregnant and Noah was born October 4, 2001. I tried to help her raise Noah, but her motherly instincts were on back order; it was too much for her to handle. She moved back to live with me in Bon Repos and began learning more English to work as my translator.

I was just starting to build Ruuska Village and invited Mirlande to be the first unwed mother to live there. Mirlande moved into Ruuska Village and got pregnant again by a man named Ricardo Pierre. One day while Mirlande and I were in the city the idea came to me to have a sonogram done on Mirlande. This was very unusual for me, as I do not normally approve of doing this test unless there is a real reason. I asked Mirlande if she would like to get a sonogram done to see how the baby was doing. She was surprised I had suggested something like that, but agreed. She knew that I never granted this to any of the ladies that requested one. Well, I guess God was telling me to do the test because she had placenta praevia and the baby would have died without help. Time went on and soon Mirlande went to a maternity specialist for a C-section. We named this sweet girl Baby Ruth, after the original Baby Ruth whom I adopted out many years before. Both Mirlande and Baby Ruth were healthy and came to live at Ruuska Village. I flatly refused to adopt out Baby Ruth. I told Mirlande that she had a safe home and a stable job; she was going to raise her.

One year later, Mirlande met Lucien and built a house nearby. Soon, Lucien, Mirlande, and Baby Ruth were all living together.

I hired Lucien as a driver and handyman for the village. Mirlande and Lucien worked well together.

MATTHEW

My life continued in the United States where I lived life not really knowing my past. Then came the elementary years when people became curious and started to ask questions. Why are your parents white? What's your birth mother's name? Do you have any siblings that live in Haiti? They used to ask many questions but I didn't really know the answers. So eventually I came home and asked my mom these questions and she answered them and helped explain things to me so I could explain to my friends. Now that I knew so much, it bothered me that I wasn't able to see my birth mother and family in Haiti so I acted out. Anger came out of nowhere and I blamed everything on others but I knew I just really wanted to visit my family in Haiti.

My parents hadn't taken us back while we were young but now that we were older they thought it would be a good time. So we decided to make our first trip back to Haiti since my brother Maki's and my adoption. My Mom, Dad, my brother Maki, sister Mae and I went on this trip.

I had so many thoughts running through my mind. I had never traveled to a developing country even though I was born there, so I expected the worst you could think of. I imagined it to be like a nasty garbage dump where I used to live. When we got on the plane I begin to feel many emotions. We were almost there when reality set in that I was finally coming home to the place I was born.

We landed and got our luggage only to be stopped by security and brought into a room with guards. I wasn't scared at first until I saw the men in the room had automatic weapons on them. It turns out they were suspicious and detaining us because we hadn't filled out the address of where we were staying in Haiti on our immigration form so they wouldn't let us leave the airport.

After my parents tried to reason with them, one of the armed men let my mother go with him to try to find Barbara outside. She of course found her and they finally let us leave after Barbara explained to them forcefully to leave us alone. That was a great start to the trip.

Outside a van was waiting for us. The driver's name was Lucien. Lucien became a great friend to Maki and me and would later become our birth mom's husband. We drove for what seemed like forever, over very bumpy, pothole filled roads, to finally reach a blue gate that read Ruuska Village.

We finally were reunited with Mirlande. How joyous we felt. It had been years since I had last seen her. We also met our sister Ruth, who lived with Mirlande. The next few days were spent out and about Port-au-Prince, the capital of Haiti. Most of the time it was just Maki and Mirlande and me. Mirlande was visiting all of the people she knew and introducing Maki and me. Everyone seemed surprised to see us, which confused me. She later explained that the Haitians believe that children are adopted to be eaten. Yes, they actually thought that Americans adopted children to eat them! She was showing them that they were believing lies, and that we were healthy and well cared for.

One day when we were driving through the markets, my brother Maki, my sister Mae and I were sitting in the back of a pickup truck which was enclosed with a cage. Barbara put supplies there and passengers when there was no room in the cab.

Out of nowhere we saw an older man start to chase the truck and shout to us in Creole. Mirlande started laughing very hard at him. "Why is he chasing us," I asked. "What is he yelling at us?"

He is shouting, "They are going to eat you!" He was referring to my white parents sitting in the cab.

I was grateful to meet our Grandpa Joseph on this trip also. He was the one who helped my birth mom find Barbara Walker when

I was a baby and very near death. He was very sick and dying when we saw him, and almost completely blind but Mirlande spoke to him and explained who we were. He touched Maki and me and expressed how grateful he was that we had come to visit and how happy he was that we were healthy and strong. He died not long after we saw him. He is the father of our birth dad Michelette. We didn't meet our birth father but hope to someday.

The days soon passed and it was time to go home. Mirlande and I exchanged hugs and we said our goodbyes.

BARBARA

Then came the earthquake in 2010. Mirlande and Lucien's house was destroyed but they and their children were not injured.

MATTHEW

About six months after we returned home, I awoke to horrid news. My mom had opened the paper only to read to me that Haiti had a very bad earthquake. I hoped that my mother and sister Ruth were OK and not hurt.

Mirlande had been driving during the earthquake but made it safely back to the village. Her house had been destroyed but no one was injured. Everyone was sleeping outside for fear of buildings falling on them from aftershocks. Ruuska Village became a clinic and safe place for injured people to be treated and to be safe from violence.

One of my friends in our school came up with an idea to do a fundraiser for Haiti. Her idea was to raise money to buy water purifiers to send to the village I was born in. The fundraiser was a great success and I was even able to show my school some photos of when I was in Haiti compared to what it looked like now after the earthquake.

BARBARA

Since I do not allow men to live at Ruuska, I helped Mirlande and Lucien rebuild their home.

I had repeatedly told Mirlande, "If you get pregnant again, you will surely die." I would not pay for another C-section and I guess she believed me because it was nine years before she got pregnant again. Rodney Lucien Michel was born on April 26, 2012. I helped her go to the USA to have a C-section and they were back in Haiti shortly after recovery. Mirlande and Lucien built another new home and were married Dec. 15, 2012.

MATTHEW

I was able to return to Haiti, for a special occasion. My birth mother was getting married to Lucien, the same Lucien who had been our driver and had been so kind to us. During the wedding celebration all the power in the house went out and it became pitch black. The generators weren't even working. It took some time but the power came back on, then off and then back on again. Oh! What a night! It was awesome to be able to see her get married, even though I couldn't understand a word they were saying during the service.

MIRLANDE

Years down the road, and after giving up three children for adoption, I am now married to another man and doing great. I have a good life now and have three more children living with me here in Haiti. I am very thankful for Barbara; she saved the lives of my babies and my life too. Everything I have is because she gave me the chance to learn and grow. My three children are alive and happy. They have good homes, loving parents to help them, and have a good future I could not give them. Yes, I will always be their birth mother, but I could offer them nothing. I am happy they are in good health, smart, and very talented. If it wasn't for Barbara, they may have died like my first child. I have been to the USA to visit Matthew and Maki and they have been to Haiti to visit me as well. I would like to one day see my third son, Noah, as well.

I learned how to work and made a good life for myself. My god parents are very old, and I provide them with food and medical needs. I also help the siblings who are not willing to work. My biological mother gave birth to me, but Barbara is my real mother. She gave me the opportunity to succeed in life and make something of myself and for my children. I praise God for bringing us together.

Old Joseph has now died. Michellet is sick with AIDS and has no success in life. He is not even a good thief; he gets caught much too often. Jail is his second home. Baby is still living in her father's house in Carrefour.

MATTHEW

My story doesn't end now but it's only the beginning. I hope to return to Haiti sometime in the future to give back to the people who are less fortunate than I. My goal is to one day build a school or village to aid children and families of those on the streets like my birth mom Mirlande was, and also to bring more sports focused activities to the kids' lives and maybe even run for a government position. This brings me to the next part of my future. I hope in the near future to be able to possibly live in Haiti short term to really get a perspective of what life may have been like for me if I hadn't been adopted.

Some of my greatest moments have come while visiting Haiti. Over my life I have become a devoted Christian and someday look to spread my views on the Lord to the people of Haiti. For I believe that the only reason I am alive today is because God had a greater plan for my life, so I feel it's my duty to spread his word to as many Haitian people as I can. Jeremiah 29:11 says "For I know the plans I have for you," declares the LORD, "plans to prosper you and not to harm you, plans to give you hope and a future."

This verse just proves that my adoption was of his plans. A plan that gave me a future and hope. So with this hope I need to spread his word to others so they can feel his love and have a chance at a great future.

BARBARA

Many times I am asked about my work in Haiti. Yes, I have adopted well over 1,500 children, but the women I help are a very important part of my ministry as well. Mirlande is my success story. Yes together, with the Lord's help, her life has been forever changed.

It was not an easy or fast process. Mirlande had to make many changes in her life. She was street wise and had a bad temper. Lying, cheating, and stealing are several skills the poor use to survive on the streets. Mirlande had to change into an honest, hard-working person. She had to seek out God and start to obey the rules of the Bible. She had to use her mind and develop new attitudes. She had to learn how to submit to others' authority and earn respect in the business world. This was not easy. People knew she could not read or write and had a natural mistrust for her abilities.

Over time, Mirlande proved herself and is now doing the work of a Haitian lawyer. At first, I went to the city with her and we worked together. Now I stay at the village. I prepare the paper work and Mirlande goes to process the papers. She works with IBESR, all the courts, and people to accomplish the job before her.

Mirlande can now drive and has her own car. Lucien and Mirlande are active members of a church and reach out to the poor in their family and community. Through hard work, she became a very well-to-do Haitian woman. The old saying "from rags to riches" now describes her life. Still, she remembers how horrible her life was and tries to help the poor. I am proud of what Mirlande has become and I believe she will continue to grow in knowledge and succeed in life.

The time and effort spent helping Mirlande develop as a responsible woman continues to bear fruit as I witnessed in her dealing with another woman who came to Ruuska Village.

Passing on the building trade

Nellie Fleury had a very difficult life. Her mother died shortly after giving birth to her. Her father tried to care for the six children the best he could until he found a new woman in his life. It is very common in a Haitian family for the new woman to send the children of the previous wife away. This proved to be true with Nellie and her siblings. They were all sent to different families as household workers.

Nellie and her sister, Aline, were passed from home to home. Nellie was the youngest child and really not old enough to have any skills, so cleaning, carrying water, and protecting the family children were her basic duties. Nellie was never able to go to school, although one of her duties was to walk the children of the family to and from school. Like so many other children in the same situation, the families beat her and showed no love or compassion. This led her to grow up as a very sad, unhappy, and loveless child.

Nellie began searching for love in all the wrong places. By age 14 she was pregnant and gave birth to Marvens on June 24, 2013. Everyone agreed she had made some very poor choices in life. No one would take the young mother and her baby in and with a child to care for she could not attend school or work.

As many have in the past she came to me pleading, "Please give my baby life." To her, this meant she did not want Marvens to be hungry and homeless and fight for survival.

As Nellie stood in my office telling her story, Mirlande had tears falling from her eyes as she remembered her own life story.

Mirlande told her, "I was raped and beaten and lived on the streets too. My first baby died because I didn't have enough money for medicine when she got sick. I had no food, no safe place to stay and no family to help me, but my life is different now." She offered hope to Nellie by telling her that we would help her with the adoption of Marvens and we could also help her change her life for the better.

CHAPTER 23

Renovations

I endeavored to keep Reach Out to Haiti mission small so that it could be a sustainable project, offering assistance primarily to women and children, but after the earthquake the needs around us increased so greatly that I felt we had to do more. Through generous donations and hard work from volunteers we were able to make Ruuska Village even better than before the quake. The electrical supply was overhauled and with inverters provides 24/7 power to the three most important buildings. These buildings are the medical clinic, house/office and the food depot for refrigeration. The food depot was totally destroyed by the quake, twisting even the solid steel door into a pretzel that stayed standing just long enough to get almost all the supplies out.

We were also able to buy and renovate "Dr. Charles' house," and build a church and three homes on Maki Island. We purchased more land to accommodate bigger houses for larger families. Two large homes were connected by a closed in patio, and the strong concrete buildings were built to allow for second-story additions at a later date. A large backyard provided space for yet another house to be built as funding comes. The color of the walls and buildings reflected the name of this new village—Blue Escape.

Barbara at the entry to two new homes in Blue Escape.
Photography by <u>audreydewys.com</u>

We currently have housing for around 30 single mothers and children in Ruuska Village, Maki Island and Blue Escape. We also have *Viera*, a beautiful church at Maki Island with A Haitian pastor and about 50 to 70 people attending. The women do not have all their "wants" supplied, but they do have the necessities to live a good life and opportunities to make their lives and the lives of their children better. One important benefit that all have is security.

Viera Church at Maki Island donated by Pat Roth.
Photography by <u>audreydewys.com</u>

These days, Haitians live in fear. It is just part of everyday life in Haiti. Hungry, depressed, angry, jealous, desperate people victimize the unprotected. For many, it is the only means of survival. For that reason, Reach Out to Haiti tries to protect its people and property with steel gates and high walls topped with razor or concertina wire.

Some things don't change

We still have a large food distribution project, and rent assistance project. Every 14 days, about 300 women, most of whom have given children up for adoption, come for food for their families. There is a clothing and shoe depot for those who need a little extra help. The medical clinic continues to dispense free medical supplies and when nurses and doctors come we offer free medical care.

We've been able to continue the School Backpack Giveaway Program. In all, we are able to give about 500 full backpacks to families, of adopted children. We try to help the siblings of the children that have been adopted. Each school bag is full of school supplies, as well as personal hygiene items, toys, blankets, clothes, etc. In order for a family to receive one or more, all they have to do is provide a photo copy of the last year's report card and a birth certificate proving that the child is a biological sibling to the adopted child.

Food and basic living supplies are always needed.
Photography by audreydewys.com

Contrary winds

After doing almost 1500 adoptions, I will be limiting this ministry to one or two at a time. UNICEF has made it nearly impossible to do an adoption for a reasonable cost and in a reasonable time. It is now costing $20,000 USD and one to three years to complete an adoption. This is not acceptable to me. It seems a shame that the women have learned how to be good nannies, but will have fewer and fewer opportunities to work at Ruuska Village.

Building potential for success

Education is an ever increasing priority for Reach out To Haiti. Morning and afternoon classes are conducted for the children who attend school in Ruuska Village. For other students that live in the villages, we provide tuition, uniforms and backpacks filled with necessary items to attend school.

Developing programs that will enable residents to be independent and self-sufficient is my top priority at this time in the ongoing work of Reach Out to Haiti. The newest programs are for the women. Monday and Tuesday we have nail care classes. Wednesday and Thursday are sewing classes at the newest building called, "Margaret's Sewing Spot." This was named for a generous lady that had retired her sewing crafts and donated her supplies to Ruuska. One woman, now with her daughters, operates a sewing business out of her home.

The nail care class is taught by one of the ladies that got married and moved out of Ruuska. She teaches the women to do manicures and pedicures, which is another skill that will generate income. Eight of the women are now able to do pedicures and hair styling. Friday mornings, many women gather to make bracelets. The bracelets are attractive and the women enjoy the lessons and time together. Selling the bracelets will provide income in the tourist markets. We next plan to teach the women weaving which also attract tourist dollars.

What goes around, comes around

Reach Out to Haiti was established as a support organization to give a helping hand to other groups. Now, Reach Out to Haiti continues its ministry to single mothers through the helping hands of other ministries. Without the volunteers, partnering organizations, and generous donors, I could not continue the ministry of Reach Out To Haiti.

Among those partners is Air Mobile Ministries. Joe Hurston continues his work of providing and servicing water purifiers, but he never arrives without diapers, formula, baby food and baby clothes packed up to his ears in his single engine plane.

The German Dental Association and Lions Club International continue to support Maki Island. Church at Viera in Florida sends 4-5 teams a year to Ruuska Village. The church assists with food distribution, playing with and caring for the children, developing relationships with the women and light maintenance and construction projects. The Florida church also provides financial support for a Haitian pastor for the church on Maki Island.

One of my great joys is seeing adopted children return to Haiti. Several who are now teenagers or young adults have returned to help Reach Out to Haiti. Many reconnect with their birth family and take time to learn more about their birth culture. They are thankful for the way God ordered their lives and recognize they were given the gift of life through adoption.

Several years after adoption, Askenia Chevalier, Mackentoch Pierre Louis, and Mageline Julien return to help Barbara. Photo Credit: Barbara Walker

What does the future hold for Haiti?

I have watched in sadness as evil and danger seem to increase rather than decrease in Haiti. People are still dying of starvation, dehydration, and common illnesses that could be cured with basic medical care or even clean, pure water. Violence plagues this country, and people are killed just because they are in the wrong place at the time riots start. Fires, floods, hurricanes, and even earthquakes, have killed so many people. No family and no class of people are spared from tragedy.

Are the children in Haiti suffering less? Are the children safer? Are the children in less need of being adopted? No! More children will die because UNICEF doesn't feed them, IBESR can't feed them, the people have no jobs, and no steady food source. Help will never come from the corrupt and selfish government. There are a few organizations that help the children in need, *Love A Child*, *Feed My Starving Children* and *USAID*. USAID and Food for the Poor all donate food to our mission and we are beyond grateful for their help and support. All of these organizations, however, have seen large reductions in donations. Without donations, they have to reduce the number of families for which they provide food. This all adds up to **more children suffering** in Haiti. Even mission organizations that feed children are receiving fewer donations due to giver fatigue, aging of previous donors, and changes in North American economies.

I remember saying every year, "It can't get any worse," but I was wrong. People ask, "Is there any hope for Haiti?" I sadly answer, "No. There is no hope unless the people reject Satan, his ways, and turn to God and live out true Christianity. It is a simple choice, 'Live for God or perish by the hand of Satan.'"

The people keep looking for a savior in the form of a new president and political party, only to find a repeat of the past; a self-serving president, with a corrupt government. They repeat the same cycle: election, dissatisfaction, unrest, and finally ousting the president before the term ends.

What can one person do to bring hope to Haiti? In spite of the continued desperation in the country, I have peace about my part in bringing change to Haiti. I am only one person, but I did what I could to make sure that at least 1500 children had a better home than the rooster I viewed on my first trip to Haiti.

I continue to do my best to help women find a better way of living and a better life for their children. I have a wonderful inner peace, a special happiness and fulfillment from dedicating my life to our Lord's service.

I will continue because the children need me

I truly believe that God has used me as a tool to place the stepping stone of adoption on the path of these children so they can follow the predestined path God has prepared for each of them. Each day I will continue to step out and follow the path God has prepared for me.

-End-

One woman started **Reach Out To Haiti Inc**.
Then thousands of people helped it continue
and grow. To these people I say,

THANK YOU!

*To you, the reader of Make That Baby Happy! I extend
an invitation to be a part of Reach Out to Haiti. We
welcome you to join us with your prayers, financial
help, volunteering of your time or donating supplies.*

Barbara

Reach Out To Haiti
www.reachouttohaiti.com
email: reachouttohaiti@yahoo.com
mailing address: 168 Gutbrodt Road, Melrose, NY 12121
Phone NY: 518-753-6618
Phone Haiti: 518-478-2383 or 509-3880-1895
Ruuska Village
Maki Island Village
Blue Escape Village

Reach Out To Haiti, Inc.,
Is a nonprofit, multi-functioning
USA 501 C3 organization.

CPSIA information can be obtained at www.ICGtesting.com
Printed in the USA
LVOW07s0133280416

485644LV00001BA/1/P